# SUSTAINABLE PROFIT GROWTH

## HUNDREDS OF WAYS TO KEEP AND GROW YOUR PROFITS

### BY MICHAEL WYNNE

Printed in the United States of America

Print ISBN: 9781735870007
E-Book ISBN: 9781735870014

## Canoe Tree Press

4697 Main Street
Manchester Center, VT 05255
Canoe Tree Press is a division of DartFrog Books.

# Acknowledgements

Special thanks to Andrea Gold, president of Gold Stars Speakers Bureau for insights and encouragement. Andrea works with top quality professional speakers, has helped other authors with their books, and is the author of *The Business of Successful Speaking: Proven Secrets to Becoming a Million Dollar Speaker.*

Only someone like Donald Wiencek, who successfully ran a $30 million company such as B&B Electronics for 10 years can know what it feels like to be responsible for continued sales and Profit growth through both good and bad times. Dons insights helped me restructure this book in a way that is more likely to meet the needs of CEOs everywhere around the globe.

Thanks to Jerry Kovach, CEO of Competitive Leadership Teams, for his very special manufacturing productivity perspective and his strong sense of how profits can be substantially enhanced through improved management practices.

I am also indebted to Hugh Rushing, Executive Vice President of the Cookware Manufacturers Association, for sharing his broad and in-depth business wisdom which, by the way, influenced both the title and content of this book.

Special thanks to a wonderfully successful businessperson, who also happens to be my wife, Janelle Brittain, CSP, MBA, CEO. She has edited the book through several iterations and has provided a great number of very productive ideas and suggestions to make this book more focused on the right things for helping business executives from many industries.

# Contents

# INTRODUCTION
# A Total Focus

## HUNDREDS OF WAYS TO GROW YOUR PROFITS!

Superman, Batman, and even Spiderman had a lot going for them, but none of them achieved the status of Superhero from running a successful business. Yet someone who is running a successful business faces even greater challenges and provides greater good for humanity. Especially during times of special challenge like Covid 19 shutdowns when many businesses are facing basic survival issues. This requires knowing all of the hundreds of ways to keep and grow your profits in this book.

My idea of a business Superhero is someone who has built a Team that successfully achieves SUSTAINABLE PROFIT GROWTH. Management consultant W. Edwards Deming was not a Superhero, but he achieved something even greater. After World War Two, his insights helped the Japanese build the super powerful economy they now enjoy. Although he never referred to his vision as Sustainable Profit, he basically defined it in the following statement.

*"What we need to do is learn to work in the system, by which I mean that everybody, every team, every platform, every division, every component is there not for individual competitive profit or recognition, but for contribution to the system as a whole on a win-win basis."*
*W. Edwards Deming*

SUSTAINABLE PROFIT GROWTH is about people; they are more valuable than profit, and no company can make a profit without them. The SUSTAINABLE PROFIT GROWTH of your business is the sum of all its profit-making talent. It is a capacity. This book shows you how to grow both your people-talent and your profits to their maximum and beyond.

SUSTAINABLE PROFIT GROWTH occurs when everyone and everything in your business is engaged in growing the bottom line. It is a result!

**A total focus on Profit** is what makes SUSTAINABLE PROFIT **GROWTH** possible. Ideally, everyone in your business, regardless of their level, would like to be perceived as valuable profit builders and customer supporters rather than just employees. Beyond just increasing profits, this books purpose is to help you create that powerful profit-generating, motivational, perception.

A worthy goal for any business, *Profit* is a major achievement you will be proud of. In fact, instead of wearing a triangle with a capital S on your chest (like Superman), when you build the team that helps your business achieve the condition of Sustainable Profit, you deserve to proudly wear a triangle with a capital **$** on it and be a BUSINESS SUPERHERO.

Why all the fuss about profit? *Think!* What Would a World Without Profit Look Like?

Unfortunately, profit has been given a bad name by greedy Wall Street brokers and, almost, but not quite, as greedy, corporate executives. But profit in itself is not a bad thing.

*Profit is a necessary good that helps make the world a better place to live in.*

Have you ever asked yourself what would a world without profit look like? That world would be a very different, unpleasant place to live in. I would be like going back to Medieval times.

Consider the following:

- Without profit, commerce would not exist. Other than to barter supplies, there would be no reason to build businesses.
- Food would not be produced for sale because with no profit there would be little incentive for farms to grow and produce.
- Merchandise would not be created. With no stores and people with minimal income, there would be no buyers, and no incentive to create and produce merchandise.
- Services would not be rendered because people would be too busy just trying to survive and grow their own food, to find the time to offer services.
- Clothing would be minimal because people would not be able to afford it, plus there probably would not be a clothing industry.
- Companies would be only small businesses based on barter.
- Technology would be severely limited because education would be minimal, and funding would be almost non-existent.
- Inventions would go un-invented because technology and lifestyles would not encourage them.
- Communications would be primitive because of the lack of technology and funding, plus people would not be able to afford them.
- Jobs would not be created.
- Roads would be dirt tracks, and cars would be replaced by carts.
- Without profit as an incentive it is unlikely there would be an auto industry.
- Cities would be replaced by villages, and houses by huts.
- Transportation would be much more difficult, and people on farms would not have easy access to cities, plus there would not be enough housing.
- Governments would be inoperative as they would not be able to afford employees, other than by raising taxes which people would not be able to afford anyway.
- Books would still be hand-written because without profit

print shops, typewriters and computers would not have been invented.
- Philanthropy would not exist because it could not be funded.
- Religions would be much smaller because it would be harder to spread the word.

Profit is essential to civilization and, for the most part, has brought progress, improvement, comfort, welfare, wealth and health to humanity. *Never underestimate the power and the benefits that profit brings to the welfare of the world.* As a businessperson, never allow others to try to make you feel guilty about generating profits, as long as you do it honestly and provide true value.

Profit may tend to be elusive, uneven and irregular, and quickly vanishes when not pursued relentlessly. But the truth is that profit is generated by the people, for the people, and for the welfare of the people.

Profit happens when everything and everyone within the company contributes to growing the bottom line. Every business should aim for Sustainable Profit Growth, because it is not only desirable but achievable. Besides, your business deserves to be sustainably profitable. This book shows you how your business can achieve great Profit.

## A PROFIT LESSON FROM PERSONAL EXPERIENCE

No one is ever promoted to an easier job. On my first job as a CEO, I was given the responsibility of running a company that had been losing money for four years. It was in a sector of the chemical industry that I knew nothing about, and in a third world country that was going through major economic struggles. In fact, the goal I was given was not to make a profit, *but to reduce the loss.*

I gathered the local team and congratulated them for having reduced the loss so far. They had done a good job but, if all you focus on is reducing the loss, chances are you will never make a profit. So, I told them that with their help and ideas we were going to make a profit that year and continue to do so every year thereafter.

Did you ever notice that when you buy a new car, suddenly you begin to see such cars everywhere, and it also seems like everyone chose the same color for their cars. The fact is the world has not changed, *but your view of it has.*

When you and your team think "PROFIT" on a daily basis, you begin to see opportunities everywhere and then – *your world will really change.*

*A company that is losing money is like a sinking ship.* So, the first thing we did was plug the profit leaks. Where were we losing money? We conducted a review of all our operations questioning costs, discounts, processes, purchases, expenses, policies, inventories, personnel, advertising, promotions, and so on.

Short term we focused on those items that were obvious, and then either eliminated or reduced them. While we did not fire anyone, we did not refill all the vacant jobs, and looked for ways to eliminate or merge them.

Then we focused on our prices and their relation to our product mix in terms of profitable versus unprofitable products. We improved the prices on slow-moving items and actually eliminated some that were clearly unprofitable; the prices on higher volume products were held level or slightly improved.

We visited our distributors and observed how they were selling our products. Where appropriate, we showed them how they could increase their sales volumes as well as their profits. Concurrently, we focused on growing our industrial clients by designing and developing new products for their specific needs.

None of these actions would have been enough, but it is amazing what the combined effect of small improvements can be. *The more we did, the more we found we could do.*

Within three months, we made our first profit and kept on doing so from then on, year after year. Basically, we did it by relentlessly concentrating our resources on the best opportunities, and by growing our strengths while reducing our weaknesses. It was complex and comprehensive.

*But the key word of the above paragraphs is WE. We did it all as a team!* I could not have done it without the talent of our team. It is not enough to just think about profit; you need to think PEOPLE. When they, too, think PROFIT, they will see opportunities that you may miss, and will help you make it happen.

To get your team thinking and focused on PROFIT, you need to share your vision and enthusiasm, and also do things every day that will motivate them.

*Our thoughts shape the space we live in, and the space returns the favor.* Steven Johnson, Where Great Ideas Come From)

**In the end, as you grow profit, you will grow and profit by it.**

## Hundreds of Ways to Grow Your Profits!

Even though early on I shared an anecdote from my personal experience, this book is not about me; *it is about you and what you can do to increase your profits.*

*Sustainable Business Profit Growth gives you hundreds of ways to grow your profits.* Every chapter contains ideas, insights, formulas, approaches, strategies, tactics, and techniques you can immediately apply to your business in many ways. However, as you progress through the chapters, *keep looking for ways to use them.*

The techniques that the CEOs, management teams, and other executives, have used to achieve profit growth are contained in these pages. To achieve success every part of your business must contribute to growing your profits.

This book offers hundreds of ways to grow your profits. Many executives may actually want to do them, but somehow never get around to it. Why? Simply because they are too busy focusing on other activities that are not as bottom-line focused.

I spoke to a group of CEOs about Profit, and was surprised

that they were not yet aware of the Profit Building Concepts and Practices that I shared with them.

Shortly after that meeting, one of the attendees returned to his company and applied one of my Profit Building concepts. Within days, he calculated that the technique he applied would save him $120,000 or more that year. *Follow the real-world practical advice in this book that you can apply immediately and will begin to generate profits instantly.*

This book is designed to help Entrepreneurs, CEOs, and other top-level executives implement those practices. Regardless of what market or industry you are in. It will also help you develop your competitive advantage. I hope it will open your eyes to new alternatives and undiscovered opportunities, and also show you the practical approaches that smart companies use to reach greater profit.

**Note.** You will notice that the book uses lots of bulleted lists to communicate information and suggestions. The reason is we businesspeople want to get our clear information quickly. Besides, long paragraphs tend to turn us off.

Another reason is that in most books, key valuable information is often buried in long confusing paragraphs. This books' bullets make reading easier and faster. These lists add up to excellent Tip Sheets and Checklists that you can use on a daily basis. Pilots use checklists all the time. You may have noticed that there have been fewer airplane crashes than business crashes. To make those checklists easier to copy and distribute to your teams, I have included them in the Appendix.

## THINK IT. INK IT. MAKE IT PROFIT.

Anytime and anything you think about PROFIT, put it in writing, share it with your team, and you will be on your way to Sustainable Profit.

Live each chapter as you read and relate it to your own business. The chapters are designed to help you evolve as you relate to the content from a user point of view. The content will help you focus on the practical applications of the information presented throughout, provided you use your imagination as to how to apply what you learn.

Situation Application:

- Imagine that you are a newly promoted CEO of a business that manufactures and sells products and services to businesses (B2B) and consumers. (B2C). Your sales are strictly domestic, that is, limited to only the markets of the country where you operate.
- Unfortunately, the country's economy is in crisis. Your company's sales are down 20 percent from last year. The number of your employees has increased 15 percent over the last two years. The cost of goods is up 5 percent, and price competition plus widespread industry discounting are creating pressure for you to lower your prices.
- Cash flow looks good for at least 3 months, but banks are tightening credit.
- One of your competitors has just launched a new B2B product with major improvements compared to yours.
- Your union's contract is coming up for negotiation in six months.
- Your Plant Supervisor's autocratic management style is alienating some of your best employees who are threatening to leave if he stays.
- Your plant still operates well, but looks run-down and sloppy.

(Do not feel bad; nobody ever gets promoted to a job that is easier than the one they had before)

Given these circumstances, consider how you might use the information in this and following chapters.

**Note.** If you are already the CEO of a business, please apply the forthcoming information to your own business. On the other hand, someday you might be facing some of the problems mentioned above, so why not try to imagine what you might do under those circumstances?

## Growth

Do companies need to grow? Yes, they do. I remember telling the president of a major division of a large chemical company who had reduced R&D efforts that, if he continued this policy, he would be out of business in 12 years. I forgot about it after a while, but imagine my surprise when 12 years later to that day, he did go out of business. (I do not remember where I got the figure of 12 years from, but I suppose there is some value to intuitive thinking.) The point, which will be reinforced throughout the book, is that *you can't shrink your way to growth or keep the status quo.*

All businesses should focus on growing and making higher profits because, *otherwise, they are destined to disappear.* The book shows you how to take the current strengths of your business and grow them to earn big profits.

Surprisingly, the biggest companies don't always make the best profit. Many smaller companies generate higher profits than their large competitors. Want your business to generate higher profits? Curious as to how these smaller companies generate such high profits? These are some of their approaches:

- Some are low price leaders,
- Others have built powerful brands for which they can charge more
- Some compete on the basis of efficiency which allows them to offer lower prices.
- Others are more innovative and offer better products and services that they can sell at higher prices.
- Some combine two or more of these approaches.

*Question. Throughout the book you will encounter the word "Question", followed by a brief question. It is designed to help you go deeper into applying that specific point.*

*Question. Are you growing beyond your initial specialty areas?*

**Ready to make a higher profit?** *When you decide to become the best, you are already 51 percent there.* The other 49 percent does take some doing, but this book shows you how, and will walk you through the steps that make the Profit journey a lot easier for you.

**Ready to go? OK, let's start with something CEOs may want to check. For example:**

☐ Do you know how to grow your profits 24 percent with just three different 1% increases? Smart businesses do it - so can you.

☐ Are you familiar with The Four Avenues of Growth that will grow your business in good and bad times? Smart businesses use all of them all the time.

☐ Do you have 40 smart ways to increase your sales? Smart businesses make sure they use most of them all the time.

☐ What 2 percent sales improvement can increase your bottom line by as much as a 10 percent reduction of costs? Smart businesses are very aware of this option.

☐ Are you aware that three modest 5% increases can grow your profits by as much as 57%? Really smart businesses know how to do this; you can learn how.

☐ What are the three key business areas that you must watch closely to make it through tough times? They are no mystery, but smart businesses know how to make them work.

☐ What is the one thing you must not do in tough times? Smart businesses do everything possible to avoid this one.

☐ Would you believe that a modest 10 percent discount can shrink your profits by as much as 67 percent? Smart businesses work hard to avoid unnecessary discounts.

☐ Do you know how to leverage your current resources to increase your productivity to the max? This is a systematic process inside truly smart- businesses.

**The answers to these questions are spread throughout the book**, but why not try to figure them out on your own now, and then compare your answers to the ones in the book later on? In addition, it is a good idea to keep the above points in mind as you go through each chapter because they help you meet the challenges that lie ahead in everyday business.

## WHY THIS SYSTEM WORKS

**In tough times, smart businesses don't panic.** Usually, to some degree, they have anticipated and prepared for them. But even then, some crises are like a Force 5 hurricane; you cannot possibly anticipate everything that will happen. *Learn what you can do to survive a Force 10 economic crisis such as the one we face today.*

**They control their fear.** It is not the fearless who accomplish great things, but those who conquer their fears and rise to challenges. It is good to be ambitious, to desire self- improvement, and to strive for better things. But it is not without fear. Nevertheless, *fear is only bad when it freezes the mind and the body.* A little fear is a good thing. It makes us quicker and agile, which is proven by how high we leap when frightened. *Learning how to grow your profits will certainly diminish your fears because you will know what to do to survive and thrive.*

**They maintain a positive attitude.**

*"In this world, the optimists have it, not because they are always right, but because they are positive, even when they are positive, and that is the way of achievement, correction, improvement, and success."*
David Landes, Historian, in the Wealth
and Poverty of Nations.

Note. Now, as the hypothetical newly hired CEO of a business that manufactures and sells products and services to businesses (B2B) and consumers. (B2C), whose sales are strictly domestic, (limited to only the markets of the country where you operate), please go back over the previous pages and see where you might apply the concepts contained in this introduction. As you do this, write down your thoughts for further consideration.

Question. *You sell products and services; but which are more profitable for you, products or services?*

## Key Profit Thoughts to Keep in Mind.

Because People are your best source of Profits

- Excellence starts with people; they are the key to Profit!
- If you want to be more profitable, look to your people first.
- Hiring the best and setting them free beats micromanaging. (Question. Does setting them free, make you somewhat uneasy? Are your people ready to be set free? Should they be?)
- Highly motivated and well rewarded people who are free to do their own thinking, rather than just being told what to do, produce more profits and fewer problems.
- No company is ever stronger than its people, and its people-strength is the product of talent, motivation, training and the way they are treated.

- Creating a motivating vision and getting buy-in, leverages the power of purpose.
- Finally, customers are people, and profits are the best sign of their satisfaction with the values you provide through your products and services.

Regarding Strategy and Structure

- Developing company-wide understanding of the Mechanics of Profit increases attention to productivity. *When people believe in something, they do something about it.*
- Planning and implementing ambitious, reality-grounded growth strategies increases day-to- day focus
- Developing profitable pricing strategies generates higher revenues.
- Designing profitable product mixes leads to greater revenues and gross profits.
- Awareness of the need to leverage resources creates new sources of revenues

Why building Exceptional Teams is essential to Growth and Profit

- Building and unleashing exceptional teams ensures progress.
- Exceptional teams grow productivity faster and consistently. *It takes a team to win!*
- It takes team effort to control costs and expenses

Innovation is the key to Thriving and Surviving

- The best way to look for innovative solutions is to look for problems.
- Innovation that creates true customer value increases marketing success.

- Today's customers constantly demand new products and services.

Two things you need to make a profit

Most books about profit are focused on finance and numbers. This book is about how you can really make profits. There are two things you need:

1. **A System.** A system is an organized way of making something happen. In this case, the system is this book; it will lead you step by step to becoming a lot more profitable than you are, and more than your competitors.
2. **A Team.** Why, because it takes a team to win; *companies don't generate profits; people do!* There is much to do in running a business, and it is more than one person alone can accomplish. For successful growth and Profit, *you need a team of talented, motivated people.*

## THIS BOOK'S SYSTEM

Most books on the subject of profit tend to be mostly about financials, but numbers, while vitally important – do not run the business or generate profits; they are mostly history. Profits come from developing talented and motivated teams that ensure the successful management of every one of company operations. *This book shows how when well-coordinated and profit- focused, those operations create Sustainable Profit and Growth.*

- **Profit Test.** The process starts with a Profit Test. Its purpose is to review your current status, define existing problems, identify strengths, weaknesses, opportunities, and threats (S.W.O.T.), and help you to start focusing on the changes that will improve todays profits and generate tomorrows.

- **The Building Blocks of Profit.** As you read this book, it leads you through The Building Blocks of Profit to the importance of thinking beyond daily operations. It *shows how to set bigger goals, and make them easier to achieve by reducing them into smaller, more manageable, ones.*

- **Developing Your Team.** It then shows you how to hire and develop the people who will help you reach those bigger goals.

- **Profit Building Strategies.** At this point, while the process focuses on the types of profit challenging situations you will face, it also provides you with strategic options for each one. As most of these options involve improving Gross Profits, an entire chapter is devoted to the power of small, but strategic, changes that compound into significant increases of Profit.

- **Pricing Strategies.** Because the concept of the fixed price is substantially weakened in the increasingly competitive global market, the book then shows how the combination of Product Mix and Pricing Strategies can enhance Gross Profits. It also discusses ways to defend prices by improving the perception of their value.

- **Revenue Increasing Strategies.** As profitable growth is essential to the survival of every business; a complete chapter is dedicated to four basic strategies for increasing revenues. Because growth can be undermined by profit leaks, the next chapter is an analysis of the wide variety of them that exist in all companies. This is why it is so important to track and control all of them.

- **Differentiation.** A major challenge in today's business is Commoditization. This is why an entire chapter is dedicated to Differentiation and the power of Perception.

- **Costs, Expenses, and Resources.** Having covered much of the mechanics of profitable growth of revenues, the following chapters focus on strategies for lowering costs, reducing expenses, and leveraging resources that basically save our money.

- **Going Global and Leadership.** The previous chapters cover the *What* and the *How* of growing profits. At this point, the book turns in greater detail to the *Who* and *Where* with Team Building, Leadership and Going Global - where much of future growth lies.

The final two chapters focus on what needs to be done to continue to grow profits as the world and its markets continue to evolve in the future.

In summary, this book leads readers through the major business areas that increase profits.

- The Building Blocks of Profit. Where Profit Comes From.
- Increasing Revenues. The Top Line Feeds the Bottom Line.
- Innovation. If You Are Not Different, You Cannot Make a Difference.
- Growth Strategies. Where and How to Concentrate Your Resources
- Lowering Costs. The Art of *Getting More for Less.*
- Reducing Expenses. Plugging the Leaks First.
- Going Global. Hint: 95 Percent of World Consumers Live outside the United States.
- Team Building. Practice: One for All and All for One, and You Will Get There.
- Leader Ship. On This Ship, You Are Both the Navigator and the Captain; You Show Your Crew the Way and then Lead Them There.
- Anticipating Tomorrow's Challenges. Tomorrows profits will be the consequence of the decisions you make today.

Your commitment needs to be steadily growing your business profits now and into the future. This will be amply rewarded in

Return on Investment when you apply the ideas and suggestions this book offers. Whatever your level in business, whether it be C-Level (CEO), or Sea Level (Beginner), it will help you Develop a vision of where your business should always be heading.

- Increase your awareness of the threats and opportunities that all business faces.
- Acquire the knowledge and tools to achieve *Sustainable Growth and Sustainable Profit.*
- Discover Opportunities to immediately apply the concepts in each chapter. As mentioned earlier, this system is an organized way of growing your profits.

*Question: Why is this vision important?*

Answer to Question. Sustainable Profit is achieved when an inspired and well-focused leadership team concentrates on helping everyone and every part of the company become a constantly growing source of increased productivity and innovation. This is your goal because profit itself generates growth with the results:

- Greater value for customers
- Above average returns for shareholders,
- More opportunities for employee development
- Builds a better world for all.

Think about it! Interestingly, just focusing on the bottom line is not enough to get you there. Why? Because, as we said above, companies do not generate profits; people do. This book explains how to increase your bottom line, and get measurable results; it also concentrates on doing so through building teams and leaders throughout the organization.

In the end, our PROFIT focus is on building a better world where everyone profits as a result of the benefits your company brings to customers, employees, and the communities around the world where you operate. One thing is for sure: it will keep you from becoming satisfied with the Status Quo, and that is good because the *status quo has got to go* if your business is to grow.

## APPLY THIS TO YOUR WORLD

Live each chapter as you read and relate it to your business. The chapters are designed to involve and help you evolve as you relate to the content from a user point of view. The content will help you focus on the practical applications of the information presented throughout, provided you use your imagination as to how to apply what you learn.

# CHAPTER ONE
# Profitability Fitness Test

## COULD YOUR BUSINESS SUFFER A HEART ATTACK?

Ever heard of a business having a heart attack? It is called *Bankruptcy*. Could it not happen to yours? That is what many companies think. If they had taken this test earlier, they might have learned how to prevent their downfall.

*Question: As you read this chapter ask yourself, "Are any of those causes to be found within my own organization? What can I do about them?"*

## GETTING STARTED

This test is crucial to your starting point because it will help you identify both problem and potential opportunity areas. As you progress through the book, keep them in mind so you can recognize the proper solutions, and apply them widely.

Business fitness is like your physical fitness. The three key areas of your physical fitness are: Physical, Nourishment, and Mental/ Attitude. The combination of exercise and diet as well as your mental and attitude management lead to a much higher level of fitness and overall health.

Three key areas of your profit fitness are: Marketing, Management /Financial and Mental Attitude.

**Marketing** is the business equivalent of physical exercise. It combines:

- Strategic thinking
- Reality-based planning

- Disciplined sales and marketing
- Constantly tracking and analyzing results

**Management/Financial** is the business equivalent of diet, and consists of:

- Management practices reviews
- Frequent financial checkups
- Cost and expense control
- Productivity initiatives
- Leveraging resources to maximum ROI

**Business Mental Attitude** has some of the same requirements as its physical equivalent, but with a different focus. It includes:

- An inspiring vision
- Sharing that vision with all employees
- Maintaining a positive attitude throughout the organization
- Developing exceptional leadership and teams
- Providing constant professional and personal growth through guidance and training
- Providing benefits and value to customers, shareholders, employees, communities.

In both physical and business fitness cases, two things are essential before getting started:

☐ Checking your current fitness, and
☐ Daily discipline throughout the PROFIT Fitness Development Process.

# PROFIT FITNESS TEST

The PROFIT FITNESS TEST helps you check your current status. The first 25 questions review your Marketing Fitness, the second 25 examine your Management and Financial Fitness, and the third 25 questions check your business Mental/Attitude Fitness.

All questions are designed to be answered with a Yes or a No.

| | Marketing Related Questions | YES | NO |
|---|---|---|---|
| 1. | Have your sales increased over the last five years? | — | — |
| 2. | Do you track which customers make money for you? | — | — |
| 3. | Are you still selling to unprofitable customers? | — | — |
| 4. | Do you know the total annuxal cost of your discounts? | — | — |
| 5. | Is your company more market- driven rather than product-driven? | — | — |
| 6. | Do you track customer retention? | — | — |
| 7. | Do you keep track of customer attrition? | — | — |
| 8. | Do you have a plan for retrieving lost customers? | — | — |
| 9. | Are your sales rising faster than your costs and expenses? | — | — |
| 10. | Do you track sales per employee? | — | — |
| 11. | Do you track profits per employee? | — | — |
| 12. | Are your total annual gross profits increasing? | — | — |
| 13. | Do you track profits per products? | — | — |
| 14. | Do you have a product mix strategy? | — | — |
| 15. | Do you avoid competing on price? | — | — |
| 16. | Do you know what percentage of customers produce the most sales? | — | — |
| 17. | Do you know what percentage of customers produce the most profits? | — | — |
| 18. | Do you know your market ranking compared to your competitors? | — | — |

| Marketing Related Questions | YES | NO |
|---|---|---|
| 19. Do you know your market ranking by products? | — | — |
| 20. Do you have an active new product development process? | — | — |
| 21. Has your business model changed significantly from ten years ago | — | — |
| 22. Do you know how customers rate your products benefits? | — | — |
| 23. Do you know how your customer base has changed in the last 10 years? | — | — |
| 24. Do you know which of your distribution channels are most profitable? | — | — |
| 25. Do you know which of your product benefits are most valued by customers? | — | — |

| Management/Financial Related Questions | YES | NO |
|---|---|---|
| 1. Do you have a discount monitoring and control system? | — | — |
| 2. Do you have a regular management practices review? | — | — |
| 3. Do you conduct regular performance evaluations and reviews? | — | — |
| 4. Do you develop Strategic Plans? | — | — |
| 5. Do your Strategic Plans span at least three years? | — | — |
| 6. Do you start your Strategic Planning at least five months in advance? | — | — |
| 7. Do your Strategic Plans include an Operational Plan for implementation? | — | — |
| 8. Does the first year of your Strategic Plan relate to your current year budget? | — | — |
| 9. Do you prepare regular Cash Flow projections? | — | — |
| 10. Do your Cash flow reports cover at least a three-month period? | — | — |
| 11. Are you keeping your borrowing limited to what is absolutely necessary? | — | — |
| 12. Do you have a Pricing Strategy? | — | — |

| **Management/Financial Related Questions** | YES | NO |
|---|---|---|
| 13. Do you have a Pricing Strategy for each product line and product? | — | — |
| 14. Do your Pricing Strategies coordinate with your Strategic Plan? | — | — |
| 15. Do you review your prices at least quarterly? | — | — |
| 16. Do you train your employees to overcome the Price Objection? | — | — |
| 17. Do your employees understand the reasoning behind the Pricing Strategy? | — | — |
| 18. Do you review your Profit and Loss Statements at least monthly? | — | — |
| 19. Have you identified the key drivers of your business? | — | — |
| 20. Do you track the economic indicators of your industry? | — | — |
| 21. Does your Balance Sheet show regular progress? | — | — |
| 22. Are all your assets producing profits? | — | — |
| 23. Do you perform regular process analyses? | — | — |
| 24. Do you hold regular reviews of supplier performance and prices? | — | — |
| 25. Have you and your team received negotiation training? | — | — |

| **Profit Mental/Attitude Questions** | YES | NO |
|---|---|---|
| 1. Do you set an example of a realistic positive attitude? | — | — |
| 2. Do you know what interests your people? | — | — |
| 3. Do you have a Succession Plan? | — | — |
| 4. Do you and your team motivate your people constantly? | — | — |
| 5. Does your vision statement really motivate anyone? | — | — |
| 6. Do you update your vision periodically | — | — |
| 7. Is everyone in your company bottom-line focused? | — | — |
| 8. Do you maintain an 80/20 (Pareto Law) awareness on a daily basis? | — | — |

| | Profit Mental/Attitude Questions | YES | NO |
|---|---|---|---|
| 9. | Do your policies benefit your customers more than your company? | — | — |
| 10. | Are you comfortable with financial statements? | — | — |
| 11. | Do you track and record statistics for all functions? | — | — |
| 12. | Do you encourage improvement in every area? | — | — |
| 13. | Do you reward accomplishment? | — | — |
| 14. | Do you recognize and award superior performance? | — | — |
| 15. | Do you and your team have regular personal contact with customers? | — | — |
| 16. | Can you define your company's culture? | — | — |
| 17. | Does your leadership style involve more guiding than directing? | — | — |
| 18. | Do you devote more time to the important rather than the urgent? | — | — |
| 19. | Do you still enjoy what you do? | — | — |
| 20. | Can you handle stress without it affecting your personal life? | — | — |
| 21. | Do you like who you have become at this point in your career? | — | — |
| 22. | Do you have a company Disaster Plan for handling emergencies? | — | — |
| 23. | Are you more of a leader than a boss? | — | — |
| 24. | Is innovation a key part of your company's strategy? | — | — |
| 25. | Do you and your team think globally? | — | — |

**Score.** 10 or less positive responses in any of the three key areas indicate serious weakness in that specific endeavor. 11 to 20 positive responses should be viewed as good. 21 to 25 positive responses should be viewed as great.

**Note.** Good is never good enough, and great can always be better. These 75 PROFIT FITNESS questions are also an excellent checklist. **Print them out and review them monthly with members of your team.**

## LESSONS FROM PHYSICAL FITNESS AS THEY APPLY TO BUSINESS

Health and longevity are among the key goals of physical fitness. What would be your business equivalents for these goals? Identify them and "Ink" them because they will become the driving force behind your Profit efforts.

Physical fitness is a step by step progressive process; you don't do 700 crunches and 60 push-ups on your first day. Business fitness is a continuing process, but it has a compounding impact similar to that of muscle building. What would you consider to be your business equivalent of abs and biceps? Discuss this with your team; it will add a little fun to the process.

Finally, you do need to rest between physical fitness workouts. The same applies to business fitness, but it doesn't mean you stop the process, but merely shift your focus to other matters that contribute to the same goals.

*Question. You sell products to both industry and consumers. The industrial products you sell directly; the consumer products are sold through retail distributors. Which are more profitable for you, Industrial or consumer products? Why?*

## SUSTAINABLE PROFIT CHECKLIST

### Brewing Profit Storm Ahead?

*Time to batten down the performance hatches, seal any profit leaks, set a new strategic course, and steer your company with great executive care and skill.*

We hope this checklist of 42 key indicators of a brewing Profit storm in a business will help you prevent a perfect storm in your company. Take a look at the indicators; if more than any five apply to your company, a Profit storm may be headed your way.

| Marketing Related | Management Related |
|---|---|
| Falling sales | Product driven management |
| Shrinking markets | Weak managerial skills |
| Customer inertia | No upgrades |
| Low or negative profit | Insufficient buying options |
| Losing customers | Inadequate pricing revenues |
| Competition with better products | Organizational silos |
| Competition with new products | Unleveraged suppliers |
| Price competition | Negative attitudes |
| Unprofitable customers | Rising costs |
| Poor product mix | Poor negotiating skills |
| No upgrades | Misguided priorities |
| Changing markets | Lack of resources |
| Selling on price | Rising expenses |
| Low customer service | Inadequate cash flow |
| Price competition | Excess inventories |
| Customer preferences changing | Misallocation of resources |
| Customer turnover | Low productivity |
| Unexciting offerings | Lacking process analysis |
| Lackluster products | Unhappy employees |
| Undifferentiated products | Unleveraged assets |
| Low comparative value products | Yesterday's Technology |
| Traditional solutions no longer work | Too many discounts |

These are the symptoms. Now, it is up to you to define the problem and develop the right solution.

*Question. Your Sales are down 20 percent from last year, and Costs of Goods are up by 5 percent, while the number of employees has increased 15 percent. Which of the arrow strategies matches this situation? What is your outlook? What should you do? What should you do first?)*

## CHAPTER TWO
# Building Blocks of Sustainable Profitability

## SHOW ME THE MONEY!
## THE PROFIT-MAKING PROCESS

Making a profit is not rocket science – but you *can* use a scientific approach to rocket your profits to really higher levels. *Profitability is a process and, like all processes, it is susceptible to continuous improvement.* It is a skill that can easily be learned and applied, and improved endlessly – provided you constantly analyze it and work at adapting it to changing business circumstances.

## KNOW YOUR NUMBERS

Numbers tell you what is happening in your business. It is important that you review your business's numbers regularly and analytically. But numbers alone are meaningless unless you know where they come from, how they are created, what is their relationship to other numbers, how reliable they are – or aren't, and what do they mean.

Further, you must frequently challenge numbers because they are not absolute but merely indicators. They are data, not necessarily facts, and even facts are not always the same as truths. Many businesspeople do not realize that numbers are not absolute. I find it amazing and somewhat frightening that CEO's and Board Directors who make important strategic decisions often do so based on numbers that they do not challenge enough. You need numbers to run your business, but be careful to not let numbers run your business. Numbers are not decision makers; you are.

Numbers help you ask better questions. Part of the great value of questions is that as we try to answer them, we discover all kinds of things we might have missed otherwise.

---

*"The wise man doesn't give the right answers,*
*he poses the right questions."*
Claude Levy Strauss.

---

Numbers are time consuming, and can be mind numbing at times, but they are the salvation of every business; they can even protect your business from fraud and abuse. *Further, numbers work better and are more productive when you share them with your people.*

So, for your own protection and benefit, know your numbers. *Remember: what you don't measure, you don't get.*

**Warning!** Once you become familiar and comfortable with your numbers and the reports that contain them, the natural tendency is to scan rather than study them...Don't! Make it a habit to look for flaws, for questionable numbers, to compare month to month and year to year, and continually challenge the validity of the numbers you receive, not because you don't believe they are correct, but you will learn and understand more by checking them carefully and asking good questions every time.

*Question: How long do you have to wait at the end of the month to get your numbers? Remember, numbers are indicators, not necessarily facts, but you need to get them as soon as possible so you can take action where needed. Perfect numbers late deprive you of the ability to take timely action. Eighty percent correct numbers on time are better than 100 percent perfect ones too late.*

## MANAGING THE BUILDING BLOCKS OF PROFITABILITY

The three basic building blocks of profitability are:

- Revenues
- Costs and Expenses
- Resources

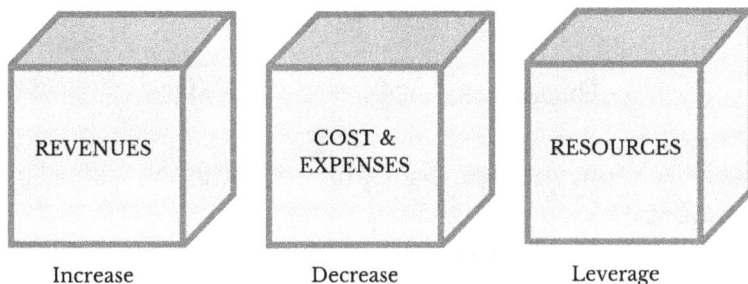

| REVENUES | COST & EXPENSES | RESOURCES |
| Increase | Decrease | Leverage |

To be profitable, a business must manage these building blocks strategically, efficiently, and effectively by:

- Increasing revenues
- Lowering costs and expenses
- Leveraging resources

## THE RULE OF THREE

The Rule of Three says that to *maximize* profits you must work with all three of these Profit Building Blocks. You can increase profits with one or two of the Building Blocks, but you will best maximize profits by involving all three. To maximize profits, all three must be managed with care and agility. The influence of each varies constantly, thus creating a challenge to always achieve the right balance that will ensure continued profitability in the face of changing circumstances

## Juggling the Building Blocks

Once you identify the basic building blocks of profitability, and how they work, you can combine and move them in many different ways, according to the realities of the marketplace and the business environment, to generate varying degrees of profit. As you work with these building blocks and combine them to achieve your goals, you will develop your own profitability approaches and formulas.

## Problems Are Never the Same

A caveat: each time, market, company, and situation will require its own formula.

*There is no universal solution to profitability because there is no universal profitability problem: each one is unique.*

Because something worked once does not mean it will work again in different circumstances. Inevitably, the circumstances in which one profitability solution worked will evolve into a new and different profitability problem. Problems are never the same; therefore solutions cannot be the same.

**The "Holy Grail" of Business is:**

*Long Term, Sustainable, Profitable Growth.*

*Make this your goal and share it with everyone in the company.*

Very few businesses actually achieve sustainable growth and profitability. A study of 3700 companies (U.S. and non-U.S. based) with revenues of half a billion dollars or more yearly indicated that only 21 (less than one percent) had sustained consistent profitable top and bottom line growth over a 20-year period.

Of all the companies listed on the Dow Jones Industrials at the beginning of the 20th Century, only one remains: General Electric and it is struggling.

## Profit, a Journey Not a Destination

Making a profit is a process. Like success, it is a journey not a destination. The process must be ongoing and undergoing constant refining day to day, year after year. There is no such thing as a "stable" profit because there is no such thing as a stable business environment. The factors that affect profitability are constantly changing. The point is to be sustainable no matter what environment or economic situation.

## The Profit Auto-Pilot

The only constant in business is CHANGE! To achieve sustainable, profitable growth, you need to design and develop a profit-making process that constantly adapts itself to changes in the business world. A well-designed profit-making process will resemble the autopilot on an airplane: it may be off- course ninety-five percent of the time – but always correcting and returning to the planned flight path. *Design your profitability flight path, build your autopilot, train your pilots constantly, and land your business safely year after year.*

## Matching Resources to Opportunities

Success in any business depends upon achieving the right balance in matching resources to opportunities. Opportunities are always many—but not all are a good match for the available

resources, which are always limited. No company has inexhaustible resources; *this is why strategy is so important.*

## Strategy = Concentration

The word Strategy comes from the ancient Greek word "*Strategos,*" which means "military leader." Strategy is what leaders do – or are supposed to do. In business as in war, strategy consists of concentrating the right resources at the right times and places to achieve the objective.

## STRATEGY = RISK

Therefore, strategy in business is about concentrating the right resources on the right opportunities. The problem is that concentrating resources on narrower opportunities always implies risk. The risk is that resources may then be lacking to attend other needs or opportunities.

The managers of a business are challenged to achieve their objectives without neglecting other areas. Armies can be outflanked in battle. Businesses can be outflanked by competition and thrown off balance by concentrating their resources too narrowly, or by spreading them too widely.

There is no magic formula for creating strategies that cover all possibilities. That's why strategies must be designed to meet specific rather than generic circumstances, and you must evolve as these do.

You must also be very clear about the purpose and expected outcome of the strategy, as well as what happens after you achieve it. Towards the end of World War 1, German General Wilhelm Ludendorf developed a strategy for breaking through the British line. The Western front had been at a stalemate for many months with both sides fighting from trenches and neither advancing. Concentrating his troops, artillery, and tanks on what he considered the weakest part of the British line, Ludendorf started out with a huge bombardment of a narrow segment of the British trenches. He then launched thousands of troops in an attack that not only broke through the line, but continued on into France conquering several towns.

Success? Yes, a huge one, but once he broke through the British line he didn't have a strategy for what to do next. The advance slowed down, the German troops relaxed and enjoyed French wines. The result? The British, French, and Americans had time to regroup, attacked the German flanks, and went on to defeat the Germans who shortly afterwards requested and negotiated an armistice that ended the war in very unfavorable conditions for the German people

What could have been a German war winning strategy ended up a successful tactic that led nowhere because he was short sighted.

**Note.** It wasn't a total loss; the Germans learned an important lesson. In June of 1940, during World War II, when the Germans broke through the French and British lines, they didn't stop or slow down, but went on to take Paris and occupy France.

*Question: Can you think of situations where you have seen similar failures in the corporate world? You may want to read up on them and share the stories with your people. Stories have a wonderful way of reinforcing important points.*

## FOCUS

Consider using **Focus** as the "North Star" of business navigation. It takes strong focus and discipline to grow profitably at any time. It takes even more to do so over an extended period of time. Strategy is essential to sustaining long-term profitable growth. Companies that constantly change strategies (Strategy-du-Jour) are rarely successful in the long term.

### CONCENTRATING RESOURCES

By its very nature, strategy must have a long-term perspective in order to provide focus; it concentrates the resources where they can generate the best returns. *Successful business strategies focus on allocation of resources to the best opportunities.*

## No Plan Survives Contact with Battle

Long-term does not mean that strategies can't or shouldn't be modified. They can and must adapt to changing realities of the market – but without losing sight of their long-term objectives. When strategy is based on a valid interpretation of market realities and trends, it may not require much change – but it will always require some. The military axiom says, "No plan survives contact with battle." *Blind adherence to any plan is suicidal. Adjustments must be made to accommodate market realities.*

## Change with Major Shifts

There will be occasions when a major shift in the nature of the market may demand an equally dramatic change of strategy. Intel startled business analysts when it shifted from producing memory chips to microprocessors. Recognizing global over-production capability of the memory chip industry and the growing need of microprocessors for the burgeoning PC market, Intel's decision to change strategies turned out to be a wise one.

**Note.** The Building Blocks of Profitability are where you and the members of your team must concentrate your attention, efforts, and resources.

*Question: Given that to achieve profitable growth, one must think beyond strategy, what are some of the dangers that you must look out for when it is achieved?*

*Question: Your CFO tells you that you are receiving an increasing percentage of small orders from industrial clients. Is there any reason why you should worry about this? And, if so, why?*

## Show Me the Money Checklist

What kinds of numbers should you be collecting and analyzing? Financials come to mind first.

- What is our retention?
- What is our turnover?

And then there is the critical tracking, forecasting, and management of Cash Flow.

Business is about money, so you need numbers that can answer questions such as:

- Where is it coming from?
- Where is it going?
- What costs too much?
- What requires more money?
- Where are you not earning enough?
- Where are you spending too much?

Then there are the numbers associated with Production:

- How much is being produced?
- Is it enough, or too little?
- Is it too costly, or not enough?
- Is it being dedicated to the right efforts?
- Is the return on money invested in production good enough, or is it generating losses?
- Are employees being productive enough?
- Is production being generated fast enough?
- Are inventories too high or too low?
- Is space being used properly?
- Is quality as high as it should be?
- Are designs helping or hindering production?
- What is the profitability of the various pieces of equipment?

Numbers are essential to managing Sales and Marketing:

- Are prices right?
- What about sales volume?
- How is the product mix performing both in terms of units sold and profit per line and per unit?
- Which territories are doing well, and why?
- Which are not, and why?
- Re: salespeople: which are meeting expectations and which are not? Which salespeople are profitable, and which are not?
- Which customers are growing in purchases of our products and services?
- Which are shrinking?
- Which customers are profitable and which are not?
- Which customers are demanding too much time, money and effort?
- Are we spending enough or too much on promotions and advertising?
- Are we building a solid Sales and Marketing base for growth?

Numbers are extremely important in managing human resources.

- Do we have too many or too few employees?
- Are we paying them too high or too low?
- Are we measuring their performance properly?
- Are they costing us too much?
- Are our benefit plans appropriate for the purposes of our company's future?
- Are we tracking employee productivity?
- Are our Accounts Receivable up to date?
- Are we generating enough cash to cover our Accounts Payable and Payroll?
- Do we have enough cash in the bank?

- Have we established a solid relationship with the banks with which we work?
- Are we planning far enough ahead of our needs?
- Are our liabilities growing faster than our assets?
- Are we getting the most out of our investments and assets?

As you can see from the above, there are many things that require tracking, analyzing, planning, and budgeting. It is vital that you devote the necessary time to absorbing and analyzing the numbers of all aspects of your business.

## TEN PROFIT BUILDING STRATEGIES

*Ups and Downs Can Sneak Up On You.* Ideally, every business will want to achieve sustainable profitability. The reality is that at different times it may have to resort to holding actions while reconfiguring the business to meet new circumstances. Long-term, however, all businesses should pursue growth and profitability that are sustained and sustainable.

The following Profitability Strategies are quite simple to remember, but applying them can be challenging.

## FIRST PROFIT-BUILDING STRATEGY:
## INCREASE REVENUES, LOWER COST OF GOODS AND EXPENSES

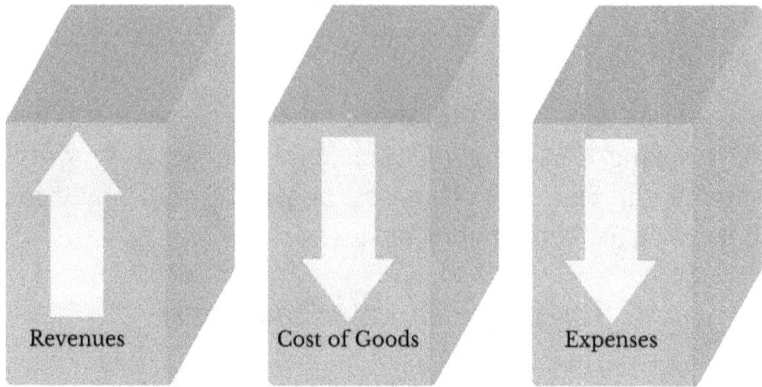

*This is the ideal profitability-enhancing strategy.* It should be the ongoing goal of every company. All too often, businesses focus on one of the three profit-building blocks to the detriment of the other two.

In good times, most companies focus on increasing revenues, and neglect lowering costs and expenses. As soon as the boom peters out, or the economy softens, they quickly lose profitability. Typically, companies don't realize their situation until they are already in trouble. Surprised, they tend to over-react with hastily conceived cost-cutting strategies that impact revenues negatively.

In bad times, like people on diets, companies over-emphasize cutting back; they cut into the muscle of the organization as well as the fat. By focusing inwards mainly on cost-cutting rather than projecting outwards through aggressive marketing strategies, they often cede share of market to more pro-active competitors.

## Second Profit-Building Strategy:
## Increase Revenues, Hold Cost of Goods, Hold Expenses

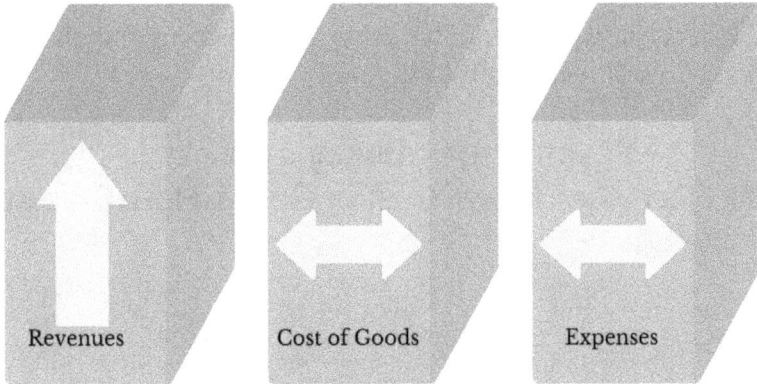

In good times, this Profit Building Strategy will grow gross profits constantly as long as the relationship between the three factors remains profitably distant.

## Third Profit-Building Strategy:
## Increase Revenues, Hold Cost of Goods, Lower Expenses

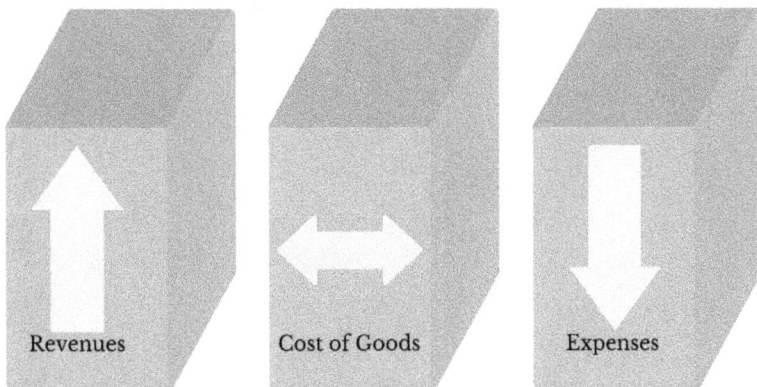

Raising Revenues in tough times is possible, holding Cost of Goods may be harder, and lowering expenses is indispensable, but if you do them you will improve gross profits. A company that adopts this strategy in good times can still be considered enlightened. Although the end result will still be sustainable profitability, *it will be a more vulnerable one.* In bad times, when revenues are likely to decrease, just holding costs and lowering expenses level will result in reduced profitability.

## FOURTH PROFIT-BUILDING STRATEGY:
## RAISE REVENUES, LOWER COST OF GOODS, HOLD EXPENSES

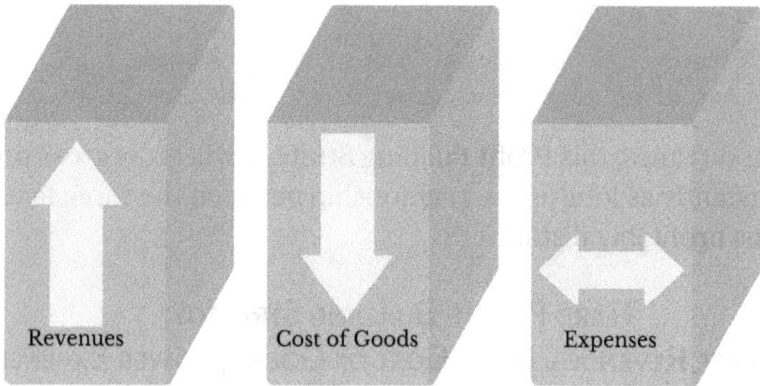

| Revenues | Cost of Goods | Expenses |

If accomplished in the right proportions, good but still vulnerable in bad times.

## FIFTH PROFIT-BUILDING STRATEGY:
## INCREASE REVENUES MORE THAN COST OF GOODS INCREASES, AND LOWER EXPENSES

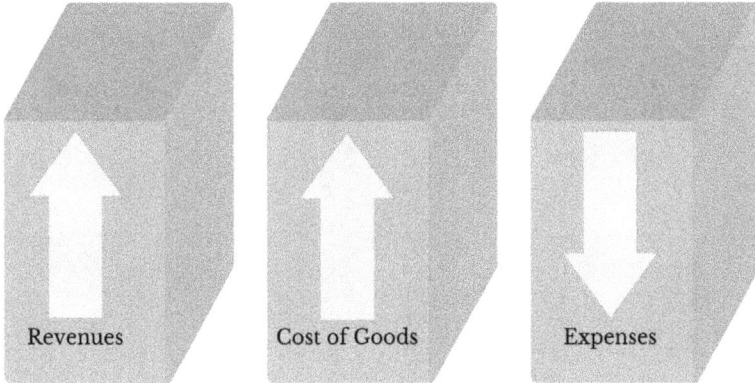

Revenues    Cost of Goods    Expenses

This strategy may produce temporarily sustainable profitability, *but the company will be on an economic treadmill.* If Cost of Goods and Expenses are increasing, the company has to increase revenues at a faster pace just to stay even. To raise profitability it will have to increase revenues even faster. One slip, and costs and expenses can quickly catch up with and pass revenues thereby eliminating profits.

## SIXTH PROFIT-BUILDING STRATEGY:
## INCREASE REVENUES MORE THAN COST OF GOODS INCREASES, AND HOLD EXPENSES

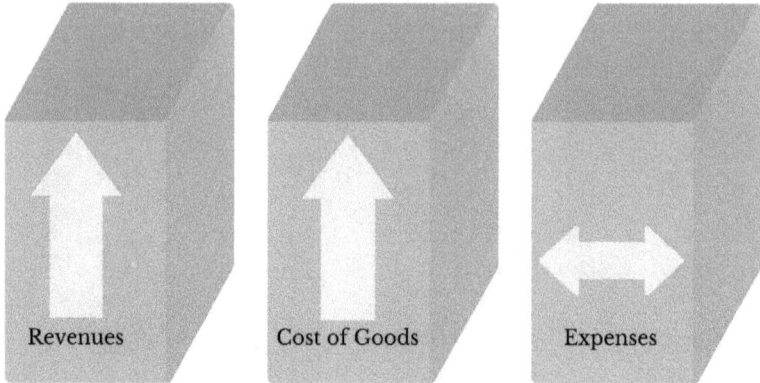

Revenues          Cost of Goods          Expenses

Done properly, this strategy may still increase Gross Profits, but only marginally. A lot depends on the respective percentages of the profitability building blocks equation. If the percentage of Expenses is very low to begin with, holding it level may not exert enough pressure on the Sustainable Profit Growth equation.

## SEVENTH PROFIT-BUILDING STRATEGY:
## HOLD REVENUES LEVEL WHILE LOWERING COSTS AND EXPENSES

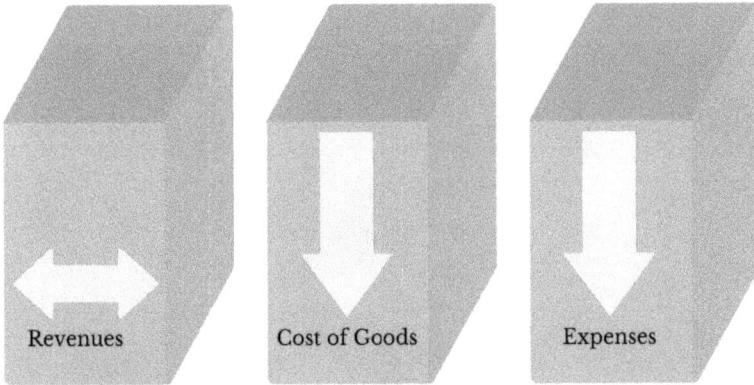

| Revenues | Cost of Goods | Expenses |

Surprisingly, this strategy will work in both good and bad times. In good times, however, the company may not keep up with the competition, and could even lose market share.

On the other hand, if competitors' revenues are decreasing, by keeping revenues at the same level as in good times, the company may actually increase market share.

In bad times, continuing to lower costs and expenses while holding revenues level will definitely increase profitability.

## EIGHTH PROFIT-BUILDING STRATEGY: REDUCE COSTS AND EXPENSES MORE AND FASTER THAN REVENUE DECREASES

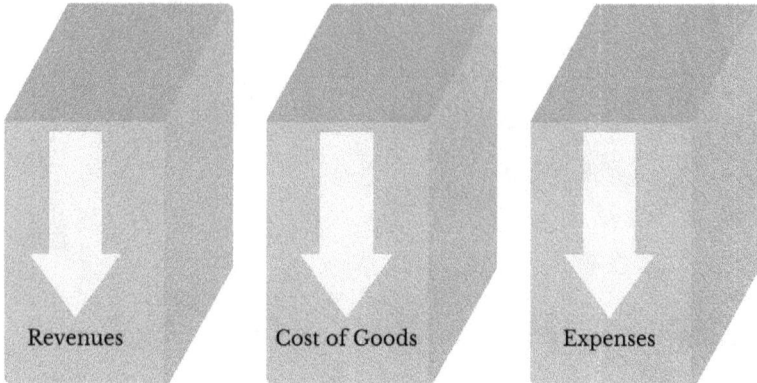

Revenues      Cost of Goods      Expenses

The treadmill is moving even faster here. Everything is sliding downwards. The problem is that costs and expenses can only be reduced so much before they reach a point where the company has to go out of business because it can no longer support operations.

Nevertheless, for a short bad spell, this strategy will increase or hold profitability, but the cost and expense reductions will soon hit bottom—eventually ending profitability growth.

## NINTH PROFIT-BUILDING STRATEGY:
## HOLD REVENUES AND COST OF GOODS LEVEL, LOWER EXPENSES

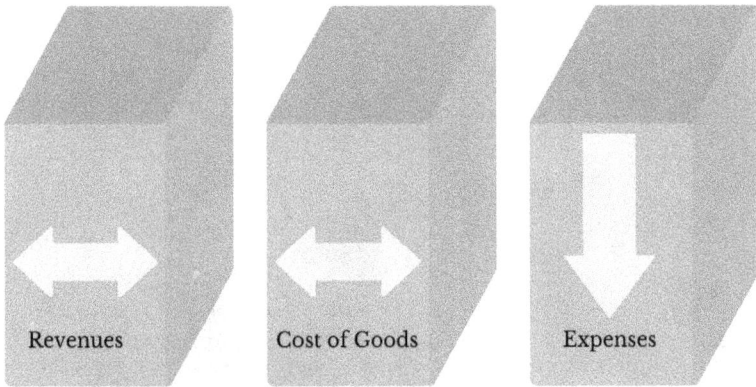

| Revenues | Cost of Goods | Expenses |

There will be times when you won't be able to increase revenues, or reduce cost of goods. So, what's left? Right! Expenses! This strategy will hold your profitability at the current level, and maybe improve it --- for a while. While you can't shrink your way to growth, you might be able to hold revenues level or maybe even increase them slightly. The problem is that you need to spend to earn; eventually, you will need to spend money on essentials just to keep the business running.

## TENTH PROFIT BUILDING STRATEGY:
## HOLD REVENUES, COST OF GOODS, AND EXPENSES LEVEL.

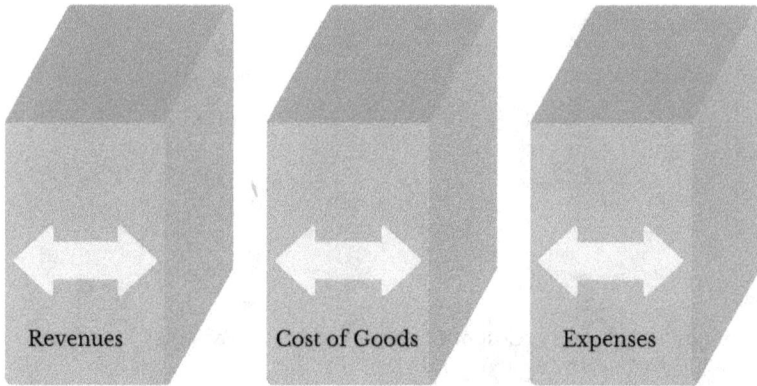

Revenues        Cost of Goods        Expenses

In good times this strategy may cause your business to fall behind the competition. In bad times, such a strategy may be almost impossible.

Overall, increasing Revenues is the best strategy and the best way to grow profits in all times. Shrinking Cost of Goods and Expenses is a good move in all times, but keep in mind that *you cannot shrink your way to growth!* Long run, you either grow or die!

## CHOOSING YOUR STRATEGY ISN'T EASY

Of course, the ideal is to have Revenues increase and Cost of Goods and Expenses decrease. But what happens when they don't all follow that pattern? How much leeway do you have with each of these building blocks? What should you be watching out for, and what can you do about it?

As you look at your P&L statements, what trends are you seeing month to month? What if they accelerate? What if they do so unevenly? Which requires the most attention right now? Where do you need the most effort? Which will generate the most profits?

Knowing where you are headed is essential to finding the right solution. But you also need to know which factors are affecting your profits and by how much. Further, you need a sense of timing; at what point does the direction become irreversible. You would be amazed at how easy it is to lose profits without even knowing it. Have you ever been surprised to discover a bruise on your body and not know how it got there? The same can happen to a business, except there you have to be much more alert to catching business bruises before they get worse. That's why the second illustration is needed. It shows you the arrow trends that result in losses.

Please be aware that these Arrow Profitability Strategies are only indicators. Like a compass, they only show you where you are going. The next thing you need to know is how to grow Revenues safely and effectively, and how to reduce Cost of Goods and Expenses without driving the business into economic anemia. In later chapters, we will describe how to increase Revenues, and reduce both Cost of Goods and Expenses. But all throughout these profitability strategies, the 80/20/80 analysis will be your best tool (see Chapter Four).

*Question: Your Sales are down 20 percent from last year, and Costs of Goods are up by 5 percent, while the number of employees has increased 15 percent. Which of the arrow strategies matches this situation? What is your outlook? What should you do? What should you do first?*

# CHAPTER THREE

# The Magic of Gross Profit Increases

## HOW TO PULL MORE RABBITS OUT OF THE HAT

The dictionary defines magic as sleight of hand. Most of the magic we see today is a combination of sleight of hand plus illusion. But real magic occurs when we transform something from mediocrity to excellence. In the profit-making world we take uninspiring businesses and transform them into sustainable growth and profit marvels.

The following set of examples shows what happens when minor increases totally transform Gross Profits.

| | |
|---|---|
| Net Sales | $1,000,000 |
| Cost of Goods | $700,000 |
| Gross Profit | $300,000 |
| Profit Margin | 30% |

In this example, the numbers are more typical of a manufacturing company. We see a business that has Net Sales of $1,000,000 based on sales of 10,000 units at $100 each. Each unit costs $70 to produce, and generates $30 of Gross Profits.

Now we are going to explore what happens when we make minor changes using different strategies by increasing Sales Volume 5%, reducing Cost of Goods 5%, raising Prices 5%, and then introducing Innovative Products.

First, we will see what happens when these changes are applied individually. Afterwards, we will apply the changes progressively to see how much more effect they have accumulatively.

## IMPACT OF A 5% INCREASE IN SALES VOLUME

This model is easy to follow. We increase sales volume by a mere 5% from 10,000 to 10,500 units. In normal times, a 5% increase in sales volume is relatively easy to achieve in most businesses. In fact, most companies would consider growing sales volumes by a mere 5% somewhat of an underachievement.

As we increase the number of units sold, we are raising production by 500 units, which at a cost of $70 each brings the cost of the additional cost of goods to $35,000.

Original Net Sales = $1,000,000
Increase 500 units X Price $100 ea. = $50,000
Production Cost = $70 ea. X 500 units = $35,000

| Net Sales | $1,050,000 |
|---|---|
| Cost of Goods | $735,000 |
| Gross Profit | $315,000 |
| Profit Margin | 30% |

$15,000 increase in Gross Profits
$15,000 : $300,000 = 5% increase
A 5% sales volume increase only gets you a 5% increase in GP and your margin remains the same at 30%.

## IMPACT OF A 5% REDUCTION IN COSTS

Ask any CEO, and he/she will tell you that a 5% reduction of costs is relatively obtainable in just about every business if you get everyone involved in the effort.

Reduction = 5% X $70 = $3.50 ea. = $66.50 unit cost
New Cost: $66.50 X 10,000 units = $655,000
Total Cost of Goods Savings: 10,000 units at $3.50 each = $35,000

| | |
|---|---|
| Net Sales | $1,000,000 |
| Cost of Goods | $665,000 |
| Gross Profit | $335,000 |
| Profit Margin | 33.5% |

$35,000 Gross Profit increase : $300,000 (original Gross Profit) = 11.7%

A 5% cost reduction produces an 11.7% increase in Gross Profit. You would have to sell an additional $116,666 to equal this increase.

## IMPACT OF A 5% PRICE INCREASE

The 5% price increase we show here shouldn't be too hard to achieve in most businesses. In some, particularly businesses dealing in commodities, 5% could be almost impossible, but later on we will show you how much impact just a 1% increase could have. Further, we will also show you how much you could save by just reducing any amount of discounts.

5% Price Increase = $5.00 per unit

$105 x 10,000 units = $1,050.000

| | |
|---|---|
| Net Sales | $1,050,000 |
| Cost of Goods | $700,000 |
| Gross Profit | $350,000 |
| Profit Margin | 33.3% |

$50,000 Gross Profit increase : $300,000 (original Gross Profit) = 16.7%

A 5% Price increase produces a 16.7% increase in Gross Profit. A mere $5.00 on a $100 product sold 10,000 times will generate $50,000. Without the price increase, you would have to sell 500 more units to equal the $50,000.

## IMPACT OF A PRODUCT INNOVATION

No matter what business you are in, innovation will be a vital key to ongoing and increased prosperity and Profit. The model we show here with sales of only 600 units of the new product, representing only 6% of the total 10,000 units sales, could bring in $96,000 additional revenues and $30,000 more Gross Profit.

Introduce, Premium New Product.

Price: $160

Cost: $110.

Gross Profit = $50 per premium unit. Units sold = 600

Total sales Premium product = 96,000

Cost of goods increase, $110 X 600 units = $66,000

| | |
|---|---|
| Total Gross Sales | $1,096,000 |
| Total Cost | $766,000 |
| Net Profit | $330,000 |
| Profit Margin | 30.1% |

An innovation product price can often be as much as 60% or more higher while its cost may be only 10% higher. The impact on Total Sales and Total Net Profit can be enormous.

## ACCUMULATED IMPACT OF DIVERSE INCREASES AND ONE INNOVATION

Part of the secret to sustainable growth and Profit is the drive to improve in every area of the business. Ongoing coordinated progressive improvement programs within the organization have the power to create enormous benefits.

Here we will show you how combining each of the relatively small improvements creates a major leap in profits.

We will start in the same order, but instead of just showing the

THE MAGIC OF GROSS PROFIT INCREASES

individual impacts, we begin to add them one on the other. The end result will surprise you.

## GROSS PROFIT – EXAMPLE

| Net Sales | $1,000,000 |
|---|---|
| Cost of Goods | $700,000 |
| Gross Profit | $300,000 |
| Profit Margin | 30% |

## 5% SALES VOLUME INCREASE

| Net Sales | $1,050,000 |
|---|---|
| Cost of Goods | $735,000 (5% increase) |
| Gross Profit | $315,000 |
| Profit Margin | 30% |

## 5% COST REDUCTION ON TOP OF 5% SALES VOLUME INCREASE

| Net Sales | $1,050,000 |
|---|---|
| Cost of Goods | $661,500 (29.5% increase) |
| Gross Profit | $388,500 |
| Profit Margin | 37% |

## 5% PRICE INCREASE ON TOP OF 5% COST REDUCTION AND 5% SALES VOLUME INCREASE

| | |
|---|---|
| Net Sales | $1,102,500 |
| Cost of Goods | $661,500 |
| Gross Profit | $441,000 (47% increase) |
| Profit Margin | 40% |

### NEW PRODUCT INNOVATION ON TOP OF SALES AND PRICE INCREASES AND COST REDUCTION

Price: $160, Cost: $110.
Gross Profit = $50 per premium unit. Units sold = 600
Sustainable sales Premium product = 96,000
Cost of goods increase, $110 X 600 units = $66,000

| | |
|---|---|
| Net Sales | $1,198,500 |
| Cost of Goods | $727,500 |
| Gross Profit | $471,000 (57% increase) |
| Profit Margin | 39.3% |

**Gross Profit has increased by 57% with only two 5% increases, one 5% reduction, and one new product.**

The equivalent of this is achievable in any business, provided leadership shares an inspiring vision, and involves everyone in achieving it.

## THE MAGIC OF 1 PERCENT ON THE BOTTOM LINE

Let us go for a more modest leverage factor of just 1 percent. This time however, we will add 25 percent Expenses to the equation, and then calculate the impact on Operating Profit.

| | Model | +1% Sales | -1% Costs | -1% Expenses | +1% Price |
|---|---|---|---|---|---|
| Sales | $1,000,000 | $1,010,000 | $1,010,000 | $1,010,000 | $1,020,100 |
| Costs | $700,000 | $707,000 | $669,930 | $669,930 | $669,930 |
| Gross Profit | $300,000 | $303,000 | $320,070 | $320,070 | $330,070 = 10.02 |
| Expenses | $25,000 | $25,000 | $25,000 | $24,750 | $24,750 |
| Profit | $275,000 | $278,000 | $295,070 | $295,220 | $305,320 = 11.02 |

Pretty nice improvement! It doesn't take much to get 1 percent improvement in each of the above areas. Think you can do it? Almost certainly. It does take skill; for example, in a tough economy you may not be able to raise your prices at all, but -- you almost always can improve your product mix by raising some prices, bundling products together, introducing new products, and other strategies the combination of which could actually raise your total sales dollars by more than just 1 percent.

If your business is more of a retail nature, the numbers would look like this:

| | Sales | +1% Sales | -1% Costs | +1% Price |
|---|---|---|---|---|
| Gross | $100 | $101 | $101 | $102.01 |
| Costs | -$50 | -$50.50 | -$49.99 | -$49.99 |
| Expenses | -$40 | -$40 | -$39.60 | -$39.60 |
| Profit | $10 | $10.50 | $11.41 | $12.42 |

Leveraged 1% approach yields Profit increase of 24.19 percent.

**Sales:** Under the right circumstances, the Top Line (sales) drives the Bottom Line (profit)

*Question: How hard would it be to get a 1 percent price increase?*

*Question: You saw the impact of a series of 5 percent increases in sales volume, and prices, along with cost of goods reductions, and the introduction of a new product innovation. Using the above model, can you repeat that series of modifications with just an accumulated one percent change in the same areas?*

## KEY ITEMS IN WORKING WITH THE BASIC BUILDING BLOCKS OF PROFIT.

**Volume, Price, Product Mix, and Customer Mix, Cost of Goods and Expenses.**

**Volume.** Increasing sales volume, if done right, increases profits. Volume benefits economies of scale by spreading costs across a greater number of units. It is important, however, to remember that increasing volume increases the total cost of goods (every unit that costs money to produce), shipping will also increase, as will the impact of discounts.

**Price.** Price is the most powerful generator of profits, but the most difficult to obtain due to competition and customer price resistance. It is important to remember that even small price increases (which usually cause less customer resistance) can generate substantial profit increases. Equally important is the fact that poorly managed discounts can have a major negative impact on profits.

**Product Mix.** This factor is often overlooked even by large corporations. Volume, price and gross profit are key considerations when planning, analyzing, and reviewing product mix. Properly balanced, the product mix can greatly enhance gross profits.

**Customer Mix.** There are right customers and bad customers, as well as profitable and unprofitable customers. Right customers are those who have a need, recognize it, intend to do something about it, and are willing to pay for it. Bad customers are those who demand much and give little in exchange. Perhaps the most important aspect to focus on is the distinction between customers that are profitable (for you) and those who you lose money on (but may not be aware of).

**Cost of Goods.** Raw materials and labor costs are the principal elements of cost of goods. Many factors can impact and affect each of these. For example, a sudden increase in price of one key ingredient can negatively impact cost of goods and lower gross profit. Sloppy inefficient manufacturing processes and technology raise costs noticeably if they are not being monitored, analyzed, and improved.

**Expenses.** Typically, these are sales and administrative expenses. An important consideration is to distinguish between productive and non-productive. What does each expense contribute to the bottom line? Expenses tend to self-inflating if not watched carefully.

## Profit Questions

These are questions that you should ask yourself regarding your current gross profit situation:
- Where are your sales coming from? Why there?
- In terms of Gross Profit, which are the most profitable of the following?
  a. Product lines
  b. Products
  c. Markets
  d. Channels of distribution
  e. Services
  f. Clients
- Why are they more profitable?
- Who are your most successful competitors?
- Which of their products are most successful? Why?

- Which of your markets are changing? How and why?
- How is your customer base changing? Why?
- What innovations have you introduced in the last two years? Why?
- Which part of the Sustainable product or service cost is the biggest factor? Why? How do your product/service costs compare to those of your competitors; why?
- How do we measure efficiency? Why?
- How do your ratios compare with those of your industry? Why?
- How do you plan annual improvements in sales and costs? Why?
- How do you plan annual improvements in sales and production processes? Why?

*Question. Due to the tough economic situation, competitors are lowering their prices. Should you do the same? If not, how can you avoid lowering your prices? If you don't, you run the risk of losing customers.*

*Question. What are your chances of raising prices? Is there any way that you could without losing a lot of customers? If so, what is it?*

*Question. When was the last time you checked the Profit of your profit mix?*

## THE POWER OF PRICING

**Smart Pricing, Even Smarter Profits.** Most of us grew up in a time when prices were fixed – or at least we thought so. Most Americans are still used to the idea that the listed price is fixed, and that we are not supposed to question it. *Well, that is changing, and you have to change with it.*

How is it changing? Over the last decade, there has been a growing trend to not accept fixed prices and, therefore, they should be negotiable. The current economic crisis has led businesses everywhere to offer all kinds of substantial discounts. This has many consumers questioning the validity of the original fixed price before it was discounted. It also leads people to wonder what the real value of the product and/or service is.

What does this mean to businesses? As consumers, in the short term we may see this trend as great; after all, who doesn't want value at lower prices? Long term, it may not turn out so well as suppliers go out of business because they are losing money, which opens the field to monopolies that can charge whatever they want.

However, for the businesses that supply products and services, *it has created what may be an irreversible weakness of all prices.* This trend will inevitably also weaken the Profit of companies, in some cases to the point that many of them will be unable to survive – as we are already seeing in the current situation.

As *a businessperson, what can you do to avoid being forced to reduce your prices to the point where you won't be able to stay in business?* The following "Key Price Strategies Checklist" is designed to protect your profits. *Keep this checklist handy and use it often.*

## KEY PRICE STRATEGIES CHECKLIST

1. Review Your Prices/Profits Frequently.

In addition to your prices, you need to review your gross profits per product or service. Do this frequently!

- Which ones are you making money on?
- Which ones are losing money?
- Which ones should you eliminate, change, or perhaps buy for reselling?
- Which products and services are under most price competition right now, and what can you do to protect them?
- Which ones are too easy to sell, thus indicating that their prices may be too low?
- Which ones are too hard to sell, perhaps indicating that you need to enhance their value?

2. Set Your Prices Strategically.

Expect your prices to be challenged. Design your products and services to fully justify the prices you will charge. Different customers may have different values; identify those customers and the benefits they value, and design your products and services to delightfully satisfy their expectations. This way you will be defending your prices even before they are challenged.

- Do your products or services target high or low-price customers? Make it clear for the consumer, too.
- Does the image of your products or services lend itself to high price? The image you create for your products or services will determine their salability.
- The price you set for your products or services will also determine their image. Low prices rarely are associated with high level product image, just as high prices are usually associated with high level products.
- It is very hard to negotiate up from a price that is low. Better to create a new brand.
- It is easier to negotiate down from a high price but be sure it is clearly only a temporary action.
- Once you are identified with a low price, it is very hard to create an image of high-level products. Would buyers prefer a Lexus or a higher priced Toyota?
- Once you are identified with a high price, anything lower will damage your image, and a damaged image is almost impossible to retrieve.
- It is extremely unlikely that a single brand might successfully cover both low and high price products.
- The decision to compete as the perennially lowest price product or service is unsustainable because there are many competitors who will cut their price below yours, even if they lose money doing so.

- The decision to compete as the highest price product or service is equally unsustainable because sooner or later someone will either come up with a better, more attractive alternative, or one that is equally attractive at a lower price.
- Actually, you may be better off if you have low, medium, and higher-level products with prices that are in line with the differences between them. It is not the same as being positioned at either end of the market.
- If you are in a market of a temporary nature such as fads, shortages or current event related, you can have a Get-In-and-Get-Out strategy with a temporarily acceptable higher price, but with the knowledge that the demand or the price will eventually decrease, and you will exit the market then.
- If you are in at the beginning of a new market, you may be able to have higher prices simply because at this point there is not much competition, but there will be before long.
- As long as your product is perceived as providing high value, you will be able to charge a higher price. Value makes the buying decision easy.

3. Charge for Value

- Are you giving away value? I hate to use airlines as an example, but remember when they provided meals for free?
- Are you providing services that you could charge for? Do you offer express delivery at no extra charge?
- What services could you create that would be chargeable? For example:
- Special delivery
- Repairs
- Exchanges
- Upgrades
- Extra products
- Parking space

- Valet parking
- Reduced waiting time
- Extended warranties
- Matching colors
- Designs
- Accessories
- Maintenance
- Information
- Reservations

Be careful with charging for things that previously were provided for free because it may cause customer resentment. How do you get around this? You do it by increasing the perceived value as a justification for a modest charge. However reluctantly, most of us are willing to pay for something that we perceive as new and improved, and therefore more valuable than what we used to get for free.

Sometimes, providing value for free is not necessarily a bad move, provided you are retrieving the cost of that value by continued profitable sales. Value adding is a strategy that helps you retain truly profitable customers, but don't waste it on customers who won't let you make a decent profit.

### 4. Train Your People on How to Defend Your Prices

Most people give in too easily when their prices are challenged. Why? Uncomfortable with the subject of price? Self-doubt? Think the competition is better? Believe the competitions price is really lower? Think that defending the price will lose the sale? Don't know how to defend price? Want to please the customer regardless of the negative impact on profits?

If you have a credible explanation and justification for your prices, most customers will listen to you. They may not agree up front, but if you continue with a well-structured defense many will accept your explanations. Why? Because they want to justify the cost in their own mind, and also want to be able to justify it to others. Ever listened to a neighbor explain why he or she bought such an expensive item? They work hard at justifying the price as reasonable.

**When you defend your price properly, you help your customers justify it to themselves and to others; no one wants to look like an incompetent buyer.**

*Question. Are your prices based on cost? Why? Are there other alternatives?*

## Beat Price Competition by Quantifying Value

**Perceived Value = Price Acceptance.** *This case is a composite of various consulting conversations with different clients. It is presented as a dialogue to make it more interesting and effective. My friend Dave was a well experienced senior executive.*

Dave told me about the problem he had trying to sell on value against competitors who sold on price. "It seems," he said, "that today's customers are more focused on price than on value."

"There certainly is a lot more pressure on price these days, but customers have always known that good value is usually worth its price. Have you tried pointing out the value your products offer?" I asked.

"Yes, but it doesn't seem to work."

"Tell me exactly how you've tried to point out your product's value, Dave."

Dave seemed a bit flustered by the question, but after a moment's hesitation he said, "Well, I tell them about the quality of the raw materials and the workmanship that goes into manufacturing a product like ours"

"Do they listen?" I asked.

Dave shook his head; "They do at first, but after a few minutes their eyes seem to glaze over. It's as if quality doesn't mean anything to them."

"Dave, I'm sure that quality does mean something to most customers. But when it comes to what goes into the product, they take quality as a given; if they believed that your product didn't have it, they wouldn't even be speaking with you."

Dave's voice rose with his level of frustration; "If quality is taken for granted, and I can't talk about what goes into making a good product, then what can I do to prove its value?"

"Value is a function of perception more than reality. If people feel the product does what they expect of it, and the price is proportional to the benefit they receive, then they'll perceive it as good value," I said. "*People don't buy products; they buy expectations of benefits. My point is — don't sell products, sell what they do for the customer.*"

Dave paused to reflect on this. Then, he said, "I thought it was obvious that good quality product will serve the customer better than products of lesser quality."

"It is, but what is not obvious is how that quality takes care of the customer's needs. Show that, and you will be on your way to proving value. Let's take a look at ways that value might be expressed. I'll mention one, and you can take it from there - and let's see how long a list we can put together between the two of us.

"Here's the first one," I said, "Time. Does your product help the customer to do things in less time? Keep in mind that the most valuable thing we can offer our customers is the gift of their own time," I pointed out.

"Mike, I don't understand. What do you mean 'the gift of their own time'?"

"Well, Dave, we can't give them someone else's time, can we?"

"I still don't get it," Dave said.

"What I mean is that any time you can help someone save time, they have something that they wouldn't have had, and now they can use it for something else. "

Dave nodded, "Now I get it."

"OK, now let me ask you a different question. How do you

quantify the value of the time you give back to the customer?'

"Unless I know the exact value of the customer's time, I don't see how," Dave responded.

"Actually, there are three ways you could do it. You could ask the customer how much time does he or she thinks using your product will save. Then, if it's in the ballpark, you could ask the customer what price he or she would put on their time. Multiply the first answer by the second one and you have the total dollars the customer would save. That's method number one."

"What's the second one?"

"You can estimate how much time the customer would save and then say, 'Let's suppose your time is worth X dollars an hour. Then you multiply the first figure by the second to get the total savings."

"And, what's number three?"

"Number three is you estimate the time saved and then ask the customer how he or she would use that time. Whatever the answer, then ask how much it would cost to have someone else do that for them. Again, you multiply the time saved by the hourly cost of that time, and you have the total savings."

"That's pretty cool!" Dave exclaimed.

"Not only that, Dave, but it works even better if you have the client do the calculations. OK, now that you've got the idea of how you price value, what other ways are there of expressing value?"

During the next 15 minutes Dave and I brainstormed sources of value.

## WAYS OF EXPRESSING VALUE CHECKLIST

Here's a list of 60 potential sources of value creation. Take a look at it and see how many more you might think of.

| | | | | |
|---|---|---|---|---|
| Speed | Energy | Productivity | Simplification | Relief |
| Earnings | Sales | Sales Growth | Gross Margin | Gross Profit |
| Safety | Security | Certainty | Loss Prevention | Learning |
| Cost savings | Excitement | Motivation | Worry Avoidance | Vitality |
| Aesthetics | Ease | Understanding | Change Facilitation | Cooperation |
| Innovation | Creativity | Quality | Operating Income | Continuity |
| Readiness | Convenience | Enjoyment | Skills Improvement | Comfort |
| Perception | Service | Reliability | Mistake Avoidance | Manpower |
| Efficiency | Information | Communication | Conflict Resolution | Anticipation |
| Satisfaction | Market Share | Share of Account | Competitive Edge | Turnover |
| Price Edge | Substitution | Disposal | Relationship | Inventory |
| Morale | Absenteeism | Productivity | Increased Value | Effort |

"Now pick out which of these potential sources of value could relate to your product or service. Then think of ways to quantify each one thus turning the value source into valuable benefits."

When Dave and I finished that day, he was smiling but you could tell his mind was busy thinking about how he would use these sources of value to beat competitors who sell on price.

Before letting him go, I offered another idea. "Dave, as you work with these value sources and you learn to quantify them, I want you to think of one more thing."

"What's that?"

"If your prospect says your price is too high compared to that of a competitor, ask for an exact amount. Then use your value source calculations to show how the benefits add up to far more than the price difference. Be sure to point out that in addition to greater value, your customer will be able to sleep easier knowing that he or she has not only negotiated a good deal but is also getting a better product."

Dave thanked me and walked away with a lot more spring in his step than when he arrived.

If you work with these value source calculations, you'll not only have a lot more spring in your step - but so will your sales. Good luck!

**Note.** What is the value of Value to you? The perception of excellent value on the part of the customer offers these benefits to you:

- Because value is more important than price to customers, you reduce the threat of price competition.
- Customers tend to be more loyal, therefore bringing repeat sales.
- Loyal customers are more open to cross and up selling, which increases the potential of more revenues.
- As a result of the previous two benefits, you increase your share of the customer, which also raises your profits.
- Loyal customers tend to stay with you longer which equates to longer customer lifetime value that also contributes to the continuity of your revenues.
- Loyal customers also tend to boast about the value they receive from your company and its products or services, and that brings in new customers.

Question. If your client simply says, "Your price is too high", how do you handle that? How about if his reaction to your price is, "You can do better than that", what would be your response?

Question. So, what are you going to do to increase your customers perception of value? If you sell to both businesses and consumers, using the above checklist of Ways of Expressing Value which of those items would work best with a manufacturing client, who produces *customized products for other manufacturers, and which would work best with a consumer who is an executive and usually works 75-hour weeks?*

## HYPOTHETICAL EXAMPLE

| | | | | |
|---|---|---|---|---|
| *Speed* | Energy | Productivity | Simplification | Relief |
| Earnings | Sales | Sales Growth | Gross Margin | Gross Profit |
| Safety | Security | Certainty | Loss Prevention | Learning |
| *Cost savings* | Excitement | Motivation | Worry Avoidance | Vitality |
| Aesthetics | Ease | Understanding | Change Facilitation | Cooperation |
| Innovation | *Creativity* | *Quality* | Operating Income | Continuity |
| Readiness | Convenience | Enjoyment | Skills Improvement | Comfort |
| Perception | Service | Reliability | Mistake Avoidance | Manpower |
| Efficiency | Information | Communication | Conflict Resolution | Anticipation |
| Satisfaction | Market Share | Share of Account | Competitive Edge | Turnover |
| Price Edge | Substitution | Disposal | Relationship | Inventory |
| Morale | Absenteeism | Productivity | Increased Value | Effort |

Now let's make a list of variations of each of these categories and see what options we have. and which may offer greater value to the customer.

| Quality | Speed | Creativity | Cost Savings |
|---|---|---|---|
| **Precision** | Design | Esthetics | Faster |
| Reliability | Planning | Efficiency | Materials |
| Durability | Production | Suitability | Weight |
| Ease of use | Testing | Dimensions | Size |
| Multiple uses | *Delivery* | *Competitive edge* | *Payment terms* |

Granted, these are assumptions, but most suppliers (you in this case) usually have a fair idea of what customers appreciate most. So, what this form of creative analysis indicates that we need to stress is **Precision** because the product is customized to the customers specifications. **Speed of Delivery** follows since the client needs to meet the needs of another manufacturer who is probably pressed for time. The product provides a **Creative Competitive Edge** in that the client gains an advantage over competitors. And because the client is willing to pay a higher price for the product, he appreciates a longer **Payment Term.**

Does this method work? It did for Leonardo da Vinci who designed it. Give it a try as an approach to problem solving.

## CHAPTER FOUR
# Strategy versus Tactics During Tough Times

### ARE YOU LOOKING FROM THE TOP OR THE BOTTOM OF THE HILL?

Obviously, you can see more and farther from the top of the hill. When your focus is on the bottom of the hill, you are likely to be surrounded by too much detail to be able to get a clear picture of what lies ahead. However, many executives feel comfort in the details and quick fix solutions. Strategy requires discipline and a longer-term view. When you have bottom line responsibility, you need to look farther ahead before making decisions.

### WINNING BATTLES, BUT LOSING THE WAR?

Running business is like a war; you face many challenges and there are many opportunities for victory. Winning all battles is unlikely. Even so, the potential for winning the war is almost always around. The problem, however, is that you never have enough resources to fight every possible battle. Therefore, defining your goals clearly and realistically is essential to keeping your priorities straight so you can choose the right battles!

### PYRRHIC VICTORIES

The Germans were not the only ones to win battles and lose the war. Talk about winning battles and losing wars, in 281 BC, the king of Epirus, Greece, defeated Roman armies in two important battles, but lost so many soldiers in the process that he also lost the war. The kings name was Pyrrhus, thus the concept of "Pyrrhic Victories" which refers to costly battles that gain nothing.

The Wisdom of Fighting the Right Battles.

- A lesson learned by great leaders is that avoiding battles can lead to success in war. George Washington lost several battles at the beginning of our Revolutionary War. After that, he avoided engaging in battles where the odds were against winning. The strategy paid off. With the help of French reinforcements, he defeated Lord Cornwallis at the battle of Yorktown and won the war. *At some point, however, you must do battle, but the secret is to choose the ones you know you can win.*
- At the time, Washington faced a far greater challenge than businesses do in our current economic and business recession. He had no money, no resources, raw recruits, and faced the best European army of the time. Anyone else might have given up. In fact, Benedict Arnold did. But, by thinking strategically and staying focused on his end purpose *Washington achieved what no one else might have!*

In both war and business, there is a time for tactics and a time for strategy. Strategy requires long term thinking and cool-headed discipline, while tactics tend to focus on short term issues.

Buzzards Failing to Look Up?

- Today, we hear many business experts advocating tactical rather than strategic thinking. Their argument is that it is impossible to predict the future because so many things are changing. *Guess what! The future has always been unpredictable, and things have always been changing.*
- That is why Peter Drucker's famous line *"The best way to predict the future is to create it,"* is still so valid. Change is faster than ever and technology is challenging tradition, improving productivity, generating new products, and both creating and eliminating jobs.

- Today we are exposed to an overwhelming abundance of "*Chicken Littles*" in the media and the business world, especially the financial industries. They can only see darkness, and even refuse to look for light at the end of the tunnel.
- Essentially, they are bogged down in their assumption that everything is so bad that there is nothing we can do about it. They tend to suffer from *decision inertia*, a fear that keeps them from doing anything to resolve the problem.
- They create their own limitations. Put a buzzard in a cage that is 8 by 6 feet but open at the top and it still won' get out. Buzzards are used to a run of 10 to 12 feet to take off; without space to run, they won't even try to fly. *The Chicken Littles of the media and industry tend to be equally stuck when they, too, fail to look up.*

On the other hand, todays experts fail to realize that although things are changing all the time, the basics tend to remain the same. The sun still comes up every morning, we still eat each day, sleep at night, wear clothes, get sick, get better, meet people, have friends, have loved ones, clean ourselves and our homes (hopefully), and need to work. Granted, in bad times some of these basics may be altered to some degree but, as we often say, "*Life goes on*".

Tactics

- Tactics are about ◻just *getting through the day*. Tactics involve immediate action, to be done mostly with what is on hand.
- There are times when tactics are appropriate; a ship may alter its course to avoid a storm, but it will eventually return to that course.

Surviving tough times takes mental discipline, self-control, patience and deliberate actions. Knee-jerk panicking generally leads to undesirable consequences. On the other hand, *wisdom is about anticipating the consequences of our decisions and actions.*

A clear example of tactical thinking is the use of discounts during a tough time. When the market is slow and competition for fewer customers is fierce, a few discounts may be wise just to keep customers from switching to other suppliers. But the effect on profits of uncontrolled proliferation of discounts can be disastrous.

*Question. Have you calculated the total annual cost of discounts in your business? Do it, and you will be surprised at how much money you are leaving on the table. In addition to reducing gross profits to unprofitable levels, discounting can affect the brand by cheapening it, and a cheapened brand is almost impossible to rebuild.*

### Strategy

- Strategy is about setting a destination and figuring out how to get there.
- Strategic planning requires defining a mission, setting goals that fit that mission, and developing strategies to make them happen. Strategies are longer-term action plans designed to achieve specific goals.

Business Strategic Thinking focuses on areas like:

- Emphasizing service, quality and value
- Protecting the brand for the long run
- Cultivating the customer relationship
- Increasing value innovation in every aspect of customer contact and experience

**Important Strategy:** Regarding customer contact, take the time to analyze where, when, how, and how often do customers enter into contact with your company, its products, and services. Then explore the customers experiences in each of those points of contact and develop ways to make every point of contact a pleasantly memorable experience. *Make customer points of contact sources of delight and anchors of customer retention.*

Strategic business leaders think ahead instead of becoming so immersed in current conflicts that may seem urgent but end up being unimportant in the long run.

According to Entrepreneur Magazine, the top 20 best companies for leadership were:

| | |
|---|---|
| 1. GENERAL ELECTRIC | 11. IBM |
| 2. SOUTHWEST AIRLINES | 12. CISCO |
| 3. 3M COMPANY | 13. UNITED PARCEL SERVICE |
| 4. PROCTER & GAMBLE | 14. IKEA |
| 5. ACCENTURE | 15. ABB |
| 6. WAL-MART STORES | 16. ZAPPOS |
| 7. NESTLE | 17. HEWLETT PACKARD |
| 8. COCA-COLA | 18. GOLDMAN SACHS |
| 9. MCDONALDS CORPORATION | 19. UNILEVER |
| 10. INFOSYS TECHNOLOGIES | 20. GENERAL MILLS, INC. |

**What's even more important is what they value most in leaders**

| | |
|---|---|
| Strategic Thinking | 67.6% |
| Execution | 47.6% |
| Inspiring Leadership | 37.0% |
| Decision Making | 31.5% |
| Teamwork | 31.0% |
| Influence | 19.8% |
| Technical Competence/ Expertise | 16.5% |

Recommendations for Thinking Strategically in Tough Times:

- Don't keep doing what you have been doing all along; just pushing harder doesn't work. Changing times demand business changes.
- Don't follow in the footsteps of other companies. 95 percent of companies do what other companies are doing, instead of thinking beyond their current situation.
- In dealing with the competition, fight your battle, not theirs. Don't do what they are doing.
- Conduct a thorough analysis of all your assumptions and then challenge them. What things are you assuming will and will not change?
- Go beyond mere sales transactions to building long term relationships with profitable customers. Aim at reaching 80 percent repeat sales.
- Take a hard look at your business model. You can bet that many of your customers are changing with the times; the way you served them 10 years ago may no longer relate to their new preferences and needs.
- Don't innovate just for the sake of generating something new. Focus on **value innovation** by offering products and services that customers will recognize as true benefits.
- Don't try to predict the future. Just set your long-term goals and work toward them while remaining flexible and agile as more changes happen.

**Note.** Include these eight points in your Strategic Planning Sessions, and you will find yourself exploring possibilities and opportunities that you never thought of before.

*Question. Why should you aim for 80 percent repeat sales?*

*Question. Situation to solve: One of your competitors has just launched a new B2B product with major improvements compared to yours, what can you do about it?*

## EXCELLENCE AND STRATEGIC THINKING

**Free Thinking and Profits**

What is the Purpose of Your Company? You would be amazed how many companies still don't know what their purpose is... or have lost sight of their purpose. Many believe the purpose of their existence is to keep plants running and creating jobs. Others believe that a company's sole purpose is to generate more money regardless of what customers, investors, and employees may think, want, or need. Of course, then there are the companies that have become slaves of Wall Street's quarterly report culture.

What Should the Purpose of a Business Not Be?

- It should NOT be just to keep plants running. Plants are the means to producing products, presumably to satisfy people's needs. *If that function can be performed economically without a plant, then why have a plant?*
- It should NOT be a tool for enrichment of C-Level executives, while employees, investors, and customers are short-changed.
- It should NOT be to create jobs; providing employment is a side benefit of success.
- It should NOT be a not-for-profit. Even not-for-profits need to make a profit.
- It should NOT be a vehicle for tax avoidance.
- It should NOT be a mask for illegal activities.
- It should NOT be a device just for employing family members.

**What should the purpose of a business be? Basically, the purpose of a business is:**

**To Generate Profits by Satisfying Customer Needs.**

While the world is changing rapidly, too many companies are not; they think and act as if they were still back in the early 20th century. Throughout much of the 20th century, companies viewed employees as unmotivated, low ROI, disposable tools.

People were told what to do, and kept from thinking or doing, anything else. Jobs were composed of routines, policies, and procedures to be blindly followed. Inspired and empowered employees are encouraged to think of better ways to generate more profits. That is the organizational model fit for the challenges of today's business world.

## EXCELLENCE STARTS WITH PEOPLE

---

*"The worst crime against working people is a company that fails to operate at a profit."*
*Samuel Gompers*

---

Most people, from top executives to the security guards at the entrance to the company, do not think beyond their jobs. Routine is their comfort zone. The goal of the job becomes to just to get through another day. *Yet, it is when people think beyond their daily routines that they begin to see opportunities for improvement of everything around them.*

Excellence starts with people, but they need to THINK. They need to have the freedom to think beyond their jobs, and constantly be encouraged to do so. *When allowed to view the larger picture, free to see its faults, and come up with better answers, people grow and so do profits.*

Profit doesn't necessarily just happen as a result of normal business activity. It takes considerable thought, in addition to time, money, and hard work, to generate a profit. But it all starts with thinking, especially strategic thinking, which, when constantly applied to the process, creates the drive and focus that generate steady improvement. Time spent thinking about your business is always a good investment. In tough times, it is crucial for survival.

You may believe businesspeople think about their business all the time, but they don't. They think about different parts of their business at different times, but rarely about the big picture—the whole business. Strategic thinking requires that you take a step back to gain perspective and greater objectivity. A General may think about troops, supplies, battlegrounds, artillery, tanks, field commanders, weapons, and many other relevant matters, but he must take everything into account when planning strategy. *In business, generating sustained profits requires strategic thinking on the part of everyone.*

**Strategic Thinking.** Strategic thinking is vital to your success and to that of your people. You and your team will save a lot of time, effort, and money by thinking along these lines. It is about distinguishing:

- The strategic from the tactical
- The vital from the trivial
- The important from the urgent
- The profitable from the unprofitable
- The short-term from the long-term
- The practical from the impractical
- The doable from the not doable
- The possible from the impossible
- The original from the copycat
- The probable from the improbable
- The necessary from the unnecessary
- The reliable from the unreliable.
- What works, from what does not work
- What must be done today instead of tomorrow
- Who has potential and who does not
- Meaningfulness realities from just numbers
- Opportunities from problems

**Comfort zones, routines and rituals are enemies of strategic thinking.**

**Questions are the lifeblood of strategic thinking.** *Never let a day go by without questioning something!*

## HIRING THE BEST, AND SETTING THEM FREE.

People investments are probably the most costly of all business expenses. Let's look at the real cost of someone making $100,000 (does not include bonus, which could add 10 to 20 thousand more salary):

| | |
|---|---|
| Salary | $100,000 |
| Benefits (35%) | $35,000 |
| Sick days ($100,000/365X6 days year) | $1,644 |
| Vacation 2 weeks ($100,000/365X10 days) | $2,740 |
| Weekends: (50 wks X 2days X $274 per day) | $27,400 |
| Effective time usage only 65% (50wks X 5 days X $274/day X .35) .350.35) | $23,975 |
| **Total Expense** | **$190,759** |

**Note.** There are many different ways of figuring out this cost, none of which is exact. So, let's just accept that this number is not exact, but it is in the ballpark This does not take into account bonuses, or the unproductive time while learning the job, plus the cost of mistakes made during that learning curve time.

**Conclusion:** The real cost of an employee *is almost twice the base salary. – or maybe more.*

**Leadership Conclusion:** You need to do everything and almost anything to make sure that your employees are highly productive.

**Note.** They will never be highly productive if not very motivated to constantly look for more ways to be even better.

## RE: "HIRE THE BEST AND SET THEM FREE."

Excellent employees are hard to find, so always be on the outlook for high potential people. Of course, you may ask 'What if I don't have a job for them at the time?

A valid point, but can you afford not to hire them?

One thing you always need to keep in mind is that you will most likely never have 100 percent best employees. This is something you need to check frequently. How many who are low performers do you need to replace?

*Jack Welch, former CEO of General Electric, demanded that every year all managers identify their 10 top best workers, and the 10 least productive. The top 10 were then listed as future leaders. The bottom 10 were placed in a limited time self-improvement program to remedy their weaknesses; if they had not improved by the deadline, they were let go.*

*Change is the only constant in the Universe; it should be a constant in your company and you can lead the change.* Of course, change should never be arbitrary, which is another thing people should be aware of.

You need to tell people that you seek positive change, and make sure it is true. Eventually, you may have to let some people go. When you do, be sure to do it with respect for their feelings and their dignity.

## THE HIRING SPEC

Job descriptions are not necessarily a good guide for hiring. Jobs change with time, and their content depends on the nature and quality of the person occupying them. As the company changes, so does the content of almost every job in it.

*When a job opens up, its content should be redefined in terms of mission, current function, responsibilities, reporting line, and expected contribution to the company mission and goals. As the content is redefined, so should the list of desired qualifications of candidates.*

There are general qualities that are desirable for all potential job candidates, and then there are specific qualities needed for specific jobs and tasks.

- Make a list of the qualities you would like to see in all job candidates and rank them from 1 to 5 (with 5 being the best) by order of importance.
- Make a list of the specific qualities appropriate for the job being filled and rank them by order of importance.
- Also make lists of the likely places and sources where such candidates might be found.
- Obviously, job candidates should be interviewed by more than one person, preferably two or three, but not all at the same time.
- Then compare notes and decide if a second interview will be necessary (it usually is), or if you need to continue looking.

Some more things to keep in mind:

- You rarely will find the absolutely perfect candidate and, if you did, he or she may be too good to be true.
- Hire people for their key strengths, rather than disqualify them for unimportant weaknesses.

If the candidate is right for the job, but is too expensive, what then? If the candidate has exceptionally high potential, you need to figure out what he or she needs and values. Then look at what they will bring to the company and achieve in what length of time to be worth the cost ...their ROI. Then, if all things line up, make every effort to develop an offer that will be attractive in both dollars and other benefits.

By the way, an important feature is the amount of freedom the candidate will have to get the job done. Do not make the mistake that many large corporations make of hiring highly talented people and then practically tying their hands with so many restrictions and so much micromanagement that they kill their initiative.

Coming back to the company where I found they had been losing money for 4 years; *the reason was simple: it wasn't making enough Gross Profit to cover its expenses.* On the surface, the solution was equally simple: raise sales volumes, sales revenues, gross margins, and lower expenses. Making these happen was much tougher and complicated. Nevertheless, knowing what had to be done made it easier to focus on each of the elements of producing a profit.

## MAXIMIZING THE "POWER OF LESS"

How did we manage to turn the business around in 3 months? The answer is: *We learned to do more with less.* When most people hear that answer they think, it was all done by cutting expenses. Yes, that was a part of it, an important part, but cutting expenses alone is never enough; you can only do that for so long before you run out of things to cut – and then what? Besides, *you cannot grow by just shrinking.*

## THERE IS NO RIGHT SOLUTION FOR THE WRONG PROBLEM

We come back to thinking it is about problem solving. *The key to problem solving is problem defining.* We need to define the problem first because *there is no right solution to the wrong problem.* Most people in business do not do a good job of defining the problems they face. They just check their shelf of problem solutions to see if there is one that fits this particular problem.

The truth is that there never can be a universal solution, one that fits all problems. Why? Because each problem is different – no matter how similar it may seem to others. "Quick fixes" not only do not work but can also be very damaging.

## THE QUESTION

The question we must always ask is: *What is causing the lack of profit?* Next, we should challenge whatever answer we come up with because, most likely, the first answer will be wrong.

## THE PROBLEM

The problem isn't to just make a profit, it is to become profit-making on a steady, continuous basis *to become Profit-Able*. Profit-Able means that the capability for making profit in a changing business environment must be in place and adapted as needed to new circumstances. You can only do this if your team is willing to. Once again, the answer lies in the quality of the people you depend on for results.

## THE 80/20/80 RULE

Profit is a strategy issue, and *strategy is about the effective concentration of resources on the best opportunities.* In so doing, it is vital to remember that 80 percent of the results are produced with 20 percent of the resources.

But the 80/20 Rule is incomplete because it fails to remind you that if 20 percent of the resources produce 80 percent of the results, then you must also address the fact that 80 percent of the resources are only producing 20 percent of the results. Therefore, it is not enough to concentrate on increasing the highly productive resources; you need to reduce, eliminate, or increase the productivity of that 80 percent of low and unproductive resources. So, we are now talking about the *80/20/80 Rule.*

We will make frequent reference to "The 80/20/80 Rule" throughout this book. Our aim is to make it second nature to your thinking and that of your team, and a discipline that will guarantee your continued success.

*Question.* Do you use 80/20 analysis to improve every aspect of your business? You should. And, when you do it the right way, you end up actually conducting an 80/20/80 analysis.

*Question.* Your Plant Supervisor's autocratic management style is alienating some of your best employees who are threatening to leave; what are you going to do about it? Questions to consider:

- Have you talked with the Plant Supervisor about his management style?
- Are you satisfied with his overall performance?
- Is he willing to improve?
- What is his potential?
- If he were to leave, would it cause major problems? (Remember, when French General Charles De Gaulle was told that a particular general was indispensable, his comment was, *"The cemetery is filled with indispensable men."*)
- Considering his cost (salary, benefits, bonuses, etc.), is he worth it?

In summary, excellence comes from people, but people who think strategically, are motivated, and improvement focused. An important part of their strategic thinking will be the daily habit of 80/20/80 analysis.

## THE POWER OF GOALS HOW TO CREATE EDIBLE BUSINESS ELEPHANTS

We all have heard the question, "How do you eat an elephant?" To learn how you eat a Business Elephant, read on.

## THE POWER OF GOALS

A goal reminds you where you are going; it also motivates you to get there. In 1961, President John F. Kennedy set a goal to put a man on the moon by the end of the decade. No one knew how to make it happen, but it was an exciting goal, clearly stated by a charismatic leader. The statement motivated everyone involved, from NASA engineers and scientists to astronauts.

On July 20, 1969, Neil Armstrong became the first man to set foot on the moon; the goal was accomplished. High goals are exciting; they encourage you to be the best. Making that decision is almost as hard as making it happen, but **once you commit to it** you have already made a great leap forward.

Goals help you stay focused and motivated, plus they force you to think things through, plan and calculate, and create a sense of urgency.

**Business Example:** I am not going to ask you to put a man on the moon, but say you run a $7 million business and want to take your annual sales to $15 million in 5 years. More than doubling your sales revenues may not be as motivating as placing a man on the moon, but at times it may be as challenging.

**Question:** What percentage would you have to increase each year?

**Answer** (In French): Dix Sept. Why in French?

Because, hopefully, if you don't speak French, you may still have to figure it out yourself. *When you figure it out on your own, it takes on more meaning and gives you a better sense of proportion.*

**Challenge:** Getting involved by trying to figure it out on your own, will help you when you decide to do something similar in the future. **Stop reading here and try to figure it out.**

*Ideally, you would want to come up with a doable growth progression that can lead to more detailed planning, first by years, then by months within the five-year target's first year. To make it easier for you, here is the progression:*

**Current year:** $ Seven million

**Year One:** Eight million one hundred ninety thousand.

**Year Two:** $ Nine million five hundred eighty thousand

**Year Three:** $ Eleven million two hundred ten thousand

**Year Four:** $ Thirteen million one hundred seventy thousand
**Year Five:** $ Fifteen million five hundred thousand.
*You still haven't calculated the annual growth percentage?*
Numbers expressed in words may not make it too easy for you -
if you had tried to figure it out by yourself.

Here is the answer in real numbers and, by the way, the percentage is 17.

| | | | |
|---|---|---|---|
| 1. 7,000,000 | x 1.17 = 8,190,000 | an increase of | $1,190,000 |
| 2. 8,190,000 | x 1.17 = 9,580,000 | an increase of | $1,390,000 |
| 3. 9,580,000 | x 1.17 = 11,210,000 | an increase of | $1,630,000 |
| 4. 11,210,000 | x1.17 = 13,170,000 | an increase of | $1,960,000 |
| 5. 13,170,000 | x1.17 = 15,500,000 | an increase of | $2,330,000 |

**Now, your goal for next year is to increase sales by $1,190,000.**
At this point, you need to figure out how much does that represent
on a monthly basis.

- $8,190,000/12 months = $682,500 (it is unlikely that monthly
  sales would divide in even numbers, but for the sake of sim-
  plifying this example we will go along with it)
- Assuming the current $7,000,000 year was also divided
  equally, the result would have been $583,333 per month.
- Next year's monthly target $682,500, minus this year's actual
  average $583,333 = $99,167, the additional monthly amount
  needed to reach the annual profit of $8,190,000.

The question now becomes, where is that additional $99,167 a
month going to come from?

- Assuming that you are in a business-to-business industry
  and provide especially designed manufactured solutions to
  your clients, it is possible that the average sale per client is

about

- $30,000, which at $7,000,000 divided by $30,000 equals roughly 233 orders during the current year, or $583,333, which divided by $30,000, equals roughly 19 orders a month.
- In the first year of the 5-year goal, you will need $682,500 divided by $30,000 or roughly 23 orders a month, an increase of a little less than 4 more orders a month will get you on the road to that year's goal of $8,190,000

**ONLY FOUR MORE ORDERS A MONTH!** That sure makes the goal seem more reachable. To reach that goal, you now need to ask your team, *"What small thing can we do every day that will help us get those four additional orders a month?"* This is the equivalent of a Kaizen approach to reaching seemingly unreachable goals.

**Think big. Set big goals. Break them down into smaller parts then figure out what small thing done daily will make those big goals reachable.**

---

*"Nothing is particularly hard,
as long as you divide it into small jobs."*
Henry Ford

---

**Basically, we have just answered the famous question, "How do you eat an elephant?" Answer: With small bites. Think about it.**

## MAKE YOUR BUSINESS ELEPHANTS EDIBLE

*Large goals can be intimidating, but they are necessary. When you don't think big, you are condemned to mediocrity. Make your business elephants edible by reducing intimidating awesomely large goals to simple, easier-to-achieve, smaller ones. You will be amazed at the power of goals, and how much you can achieve* when you simplify them. Why not set a goal right now? This book provides you with wonderful, easy-to- prepare, Edible Business Elephant Goal recipes.

Question. What big goal would you like to achieve? Now, try breaking it down into smaller parts, and find what small things you can do daily that will make that goal easier.

# CHAPTER FIVE
# Increasing Revenues

---

*"Because its reason for being is to create customers,
a company has two – and only these two – functions:
Marketing and Innovation. Marketing is the only and
most distinctive function of a company."*
Peter Drucker

---

## FILL YOUR PROFIT GLASS FROM THE TOP

*The only source of revenue is the customer. Everyone else in the company, including the CEO, is an expense.*

## REVENUE GROWTH

*The bottom line starts at the top. Sustained bottom line growth is impossible without top line growth.* Revenue growth is essential to Profit growth. By itself, however, revenue growth does not guarantee Profit; still, *without it, Profit is unsustainable.*

Can a company decide to not grow? Of course, but that decision means it is letting the competition fill the gap as the market grows. In ever-changing markets, companies that do not grow will find it increasingly difficult to compete. *The decision to not grow is the equivalent of a death sentence; it is not a matter of "if" but of "when" the end will come.*

Many companies have tried to save themselves into prosperity through drastic reductions of costs and expenses only to find that, at best, this is a holding strategy.

In the long run, there is no choice; *companies must grow their revenues to remain profitable.*

There are two basic ways of increasing revenues:

- Increase Existing Revenue Streams
- Create New Revenue Streams.

Between them, they lead us to:

The **Five Avenues of Revenue Growth.** Just as you would not put all your investments in one kind of stock, you do not want to devote all your time and resources to just one marketing strategy. To achieve and Sustain Profit, it is essential to have a balanced portfolio of growth strategies. Why, because they all offer the potential of growth and Profit, and because a diversified portfolio is more resistant to economic cycle volatility and thus more Sustainable. We will look at four basic growth strategies that encompass targeting existing and new customers with existing and new products.

Increase Existing Revenue Streams:

- Sell more to existing markets
- Sell upgrades of current products to existing markets
- Sell new products to existing markets

Create New Revenue Streams

- Sell existing products to new markets
- Sell new products/services to new markets

## INCREASE EXISTING REVENUE STREAMS

Increasing current revenue streams is the best way to start on the road to prosperity. *Ideally, 80 percent of sales should be repeat* business, *in fact, 80% of your sales may come from 20% of your cus-tomers*. Both customer retention and expansion are essential to Profit.

When developing their annual profit plans, companies often forget that *most businesses will lose around 10 percent of their cus-tomers every year just through normal attrition*. Sales forecasts should take this potential loss into account.

Given this likelihood, *the average business will start the year 10 percent behind where it was at the end of the previous year*. On the other hand, a 10 percent reduction in customer attrition can stim-ulate a growing company growth rate by 5 to 10 percent.

## How can we increase current revenue streams?

### 1. Sell more existing products/services to existing markets.

A *bird in the hand is worth more than two in the bush*. The fastest way to increase Sustainable sales by 10 percent is to sell 10 percent more to existing customers. In fact, growing *share of customer -- not market share* - may be the best way to increase market share – and more profitable too.

It costs more to acquire new customers than to grow existing ones. Yet most businesses tend to take existing customers for granted, concentrating their resources instead on acquiring new ones. *No customer should ever be taken for granted. Be loyal to your existing customers, and they will make it worth your while.*

### 2. Upgrades

Small changes in a product can be marketed as upgrades. In todays, fast moving markets, customers have grown used to the concept of the upgrade. They expect suppliers to constantly develop improved versions of their products. Even though they know that upgrades are modifications of existing products, con-sumers tend to view them as new products.

Not every new product has to be completely new. In music there is a concept called "variations on a theme." Genius and innovation are often just clever variations on a theme, a product or service. Many companies have developed highly successful strategies based on this concept. SONY Corporation created close to 150 variations of its very successful Walkman product. 3M produces and sells an almost infinite number of variations of its Post-Its. Apple offers iPhone, iPod, iTunes and iPad and it continues.

Sometimes even a small variation of an existing product can generate surprising results. One of the best examples of selling more to the same customers is a company in Japan. The product is MSG (Mono Sodium Glutamate), a condiment used widely in Asian countries. The product is packed in a round cylinder, similar to a saltshaker, except that it has a single hole at the top for pouring the MSG out. The company was concerned that younger generations were developing a preference for Western foods, and consequently were consuming less MSG. After much analysis and brainstorming, the company executives came up with a solution that doubled their sales immediately. The solution was stunningly simple and brilliant: *the company doubled the size of the hole at the top of the shaker.* The same number of customers now consumed more every time they used the shaker.

Just because your product sells well, don't think it can't stand improvement. Intel could have rested on its laurels with its original chips; they were very successful and profitable products. Instead, Intel chose to obsolete its own chips by progressing to the Pentium and beyond. *Even these products have undergone several upgrades to date. Today's customers are waiting for your new products. Don't disappoint them!*

## 3. Sell new products/services to existing markets.

New products and services generally involve two different types of innovation. The most common offers sustaining improvements of existing products. Most successful companies constantly improve their products and services as a way to raise prices and improve profits. They also look for innovations that open new niches and market segments; these are considered —disruptive" innovations because they often break away from existing products and markets and could represent the future of the business.

### Important Concept: The Customer Funnel

Think of each customer as a market channel. A channel is like a funnel in that, if you wish, you can pour only a drop through it. Or, you can pour a steady stream that will fill the receptacle as much as you want to.

The customer can absorb more than just one product. *If you move only one product through that channel, you are probably not leveraging your customer relationship.* Your customer has many more needs and wants than your one product can satisfy. Your current product or service – and variations thereof probably have many more alternative ways of creating additional satisfaction for your customers

How can you create new sources of revenue? Create New Markets

### 4. Sell existing products/services to new markets.

Have you exhausted all the possible markets for your product? If customers in one market need and want your product or service, they most likely will do so in markets where you have not yet offered it. New markets can be geographic; for example, Disney first opened Disneyland in California, then Disneyworld in Florida, then to other countries like Hong Kong, Paris, China and it goes on.

New markets can be demographic, that is, groups of people presently not served by your product. There may be additional groups of customers whose special needs could be better satisfied by your present products. Sometimes a little re-designing to meet their unique needs can create an entirely new concept. Travel has been around for a long time, but one organization, Elderhostel, created a very successful concept by focusing on developing combined inexpensive travel and education vacations for senior citizens.

New markets can result from a new use of your product that is discovered by consumers. Avon launched a skin cream for women that sold reasonably well to start with. But it really took off when it was discovered that it was also an excellent mosquito repellent for children

*Always be on the lookout for new segments and niches for your products and services. They're out there and you will discover them – provided that you're looking for them.*

### 5. Sell new products/services to new markets.

Investing in research and development of new products/services is a must for both maintaining and growing your profit. Often when companies look to cut costs, they cut R&D. Competition will eat you alive if your company isn't creating new products and even disrupting the market.

Many U.S. businesses think only in terms of the domestic market. In the age of global markets, why limit new or existing products and services to just one geographic market? The urge to upgrade has become a worldwide consumer trend; take advantage of it. Learn from Microsoft. They constantly introduce upgrades of existing products and promote them as new products.

It is also easy to think of our market as composed of only traditional customers. Where would Coca-Cola and Nike be if they only targeted the youth market? In fact, these companies – as well as many other top brand names – generate over 60 percent of their revenues outside the United States. International markets are often hungrier for new products than our domestics.

## TIP SHEET: 48 SMART WAYS TO INCREASE YOUR SALES

1.  Increase share of existing customers
2.  Offer volume incentives to existing clients
3.  Offer prompt payment incentives to same clients
4.  Increase order/unit size
5.  Deliver faster
6.  Reposition existing product concept
7.  Combine with other products/services
8.  Create subcategories of existing products/services
9.  Offer discounts to existing customers
10. Lower price
11. Add value
12. Develop new uses for existing products/services
13. Rename existing products.
14. Train clients in better and additional usage
15. Offer credit incentives to existing customers
16. Increase advertising
17. Increase promotion
18. Tele-Market to existing clients
19. Track usage and offer reminders
20. Manage client's inventory
21. Produce/assemble product at customer site
22. Increase number and frequency of sales calls
23. Help clients sell what they buy from you
24. Offer advertising and promotion co-ops.
25. Change packaging
26. Develop modified versions of specific products/services for other uses
27. Offer technology upgrades
28. Create new packaging sizes
29. Bundle products/services
30. Un-bundle others
31. Develop products/services for new price levels

32. Piggyback products made by others with yours
33. Increase information content of existing products
34. Add-on to existing products creating new categories
35. Create new brands
36. Customize existing products to existing customers
37. Offer same customized version for other existing customers
38. Consider "downstream" products and services
39. Ask customers what improvements they would like
40. Offer customers the capability to make their own version of your product
41. Create special occasion, one-time-only event, versions of products
42. Develop successor, "son-of" products
43. Develop products that perform several functions - Swiss Army Knife approach
44. Increase number of features of existing products
45. Develop new products and new uses to go with them.
46. Offer products/services in new areas
47. Export
48. Find new users for existing products

## REVENUE-GROWING STRATEGIES

**Innovate or Evaporate!**

Innovate your way to business growth! A study of 399 companies by Price Waterhouse Coopers indicated that the proportion of new products and services is a key indicator of corporate success, both in terms of revenue improvement and total shareholder return. Before the 2008 financial crisis Citigroup's leading businesses routinely generated 15 to 20 percent of their revenues from products that they had introduced in the previous two years. Colgate Palmolive generates 38 percent of its revenues from products launched in the last five years.

## INNOVATION LESSON FROM OVERSEAS EXPERIENCE

One of my overseas experiences as CEO was running a paint company. We produced and marketed both industrial and residential paints. The biggest market was residential, and the products were house paints, of which, white was the most popular color. The products were packaged primarily in one gallon, quarter gallon, and five-gallon cans.

One Friday we got word that the government had shut down the importation of the metal that was used to make the paint cans. Without cans we and all other paint companies in that country were out of business overnight!

Of course, over the weekend my brain was working overtime trying to find a solution to this devastating problem What were our options? Cardboard containers? There was a shortage of container cardboard. Plastic containers? None available. Glass containers? Can you imagine the mess a broken bottle of paint would create?

On Sunday, my wife asked me to stop by the local supermarket and pick up a carton of milk. When I got there, I discovered that they couldn't get milk cartons. Then, I saw something that amazed me; they were selling milk in heat-sealed plastic bags! I thought – if they can do that with milk, why can't we do it with paint?

On Monday, I posed that question to our Technical Director. He answered, "Are you crazy? Paint is far heavier than milk. How would you ship paint-filled plastic bags in trucks? There is no plastic that could handle that."

That was discouraging, but our situation was so desperate that I said, "Could you at least try a few plastic bags just to see if might work?"

He frowned, but said, "Okay, I'll try it".

Each day of that week he would try a different plastic, convert it into a bag, seal it with heat and then drop it on the floor to see if it could survive. Of course, the bags broke and they stained his shoes with white paint. Every morning I would enter the laboratory, take a look at his shoes, and would know that another plastic had failed.

On Friday, before I could go to the laboratory, the technical director walked into my office; he was smiling and his shoes were black! "You did it", I shouted.

He nodded in agreement; he had found a plastic that would survive the test. But then, I remembered his comments about shipping. "That is great I said, but we still have to figure out how to ship it."

He smiled again and said, "I have solution for that too."

"You do? What is it?"

"You will notice that I had to buy new shoes. That is the solution."

"Ship them in shoes?!" I asked.

He laughed. "No. Ship them in shoe boxes."

We tested shipping heat sealed plastic bags of paint in shoe boxes, and it worked. We then consulted with the distributors who were as desperate as we were, and they said, "Let's do it." We did it and for three months until the government reopened the importation of paint can metal, we owned the market selling more paint than ever and boosting profits way beyond anything we had achieved before.

Lesson learned: the only limit to what we can do is in our imagination. Our left brains suffocate seemingly wild ideas before we actually think them through. Great ideas are often the conjuncture of the most absurd opposites.

So if we could ship successfully paint in plastic bags, you can do anything. (A word of advice: it is not a long-term solution, but it was an excellent short-term one.)

Innovation is the best approach to developing competitive edges even in the worst of crises. Crises will show up in your business and innovation will be the key to surviving and even thriving.

## INNOVATE IN EVERY AREA OF YOUR BUSINESS

Every aspect of your business is susceptible to improvement through innovation. At every step of your contact with customers ask, "How can we do this better?"

Think of your situation this way: If you are giving your customers the same today as you did yesterday, you're giving them less—and they know it. You owe it to your customers and to yourself to constantly be searching for ways to improve upon the present.

Keep in mind that today's customers have learned to expect constant product and service improvements at increasingly lower prices. The only way to achieve this is through constant innovation, the relentless pursuit of better outcomes.

## INNOVATION AND YOU

*The hardest thing to do is to see your business with new eyes.* There are many techniques for firing up our creative juices: brainstorming, daydreaming, word associations, "what if" sessions, goal setting, scenario planning, future mapping, mind mapping, and others. They all work to one degree or another. Find the right ones for you and make them a regularly scheduled part of your work rituals and discussions.

Creating new approaches, products, services, and promotions, is not an easy task. If it were, everyone would do it all the time. As with so many other efforts, persistence pays off when trying to generate *new, innovative strategic options* for a business. These options are strategic in that by creating a focus on innovation they help you concentrate your team's efforts on carefully selected goals and targets. The following Creative Process offers a workable progressive system for generating new ideas, products, services, etc.

## THE INNOVATIVE STRATEGIC OPTIONS CREATIVE PROCESS

1. Meet regularly with a team of colleagues, preferably from different functions.
2. Devote a creative session to each of the strategic options listed below.
3. Generate as many ideas – no matter how wild or crazy – before moving on to the practicalities of their feasibility or implementation.
4. Once the idea list is completed, establish the criteria for selecting new product candidates.
5. Analyze each option in terms of its potential. Do not discard ideas simply because they may seem impossible at first glance. Keep an open mind. Ask a lot of "What- ifs?". Prioritize the list of selected new product candidates in terms of their ability to meet the established criteria.
6. Assign each of the top 5-10 ideas to individual members of the team for feasibility assessment and recommendations.
7. Select 3 to 5 of the new product candidates recommended for implementation and set up teams for their development and commercialization.
8. Ask each team to set a deadline for completion of its project.
9. Hand off completed developed products to multidiscipline teams for production and marketing launch.

## CREATIVE THINKING EXERCISE

To get you thinking going along creative lines, here is a puzzle to challenge your right brain. By drawing only two straight lines create 3 groups of 4 numbers.

Now, see if you can create 4 groups of 3 numbers with only two straight lines. The solution to both puzzles are in the Appendix.

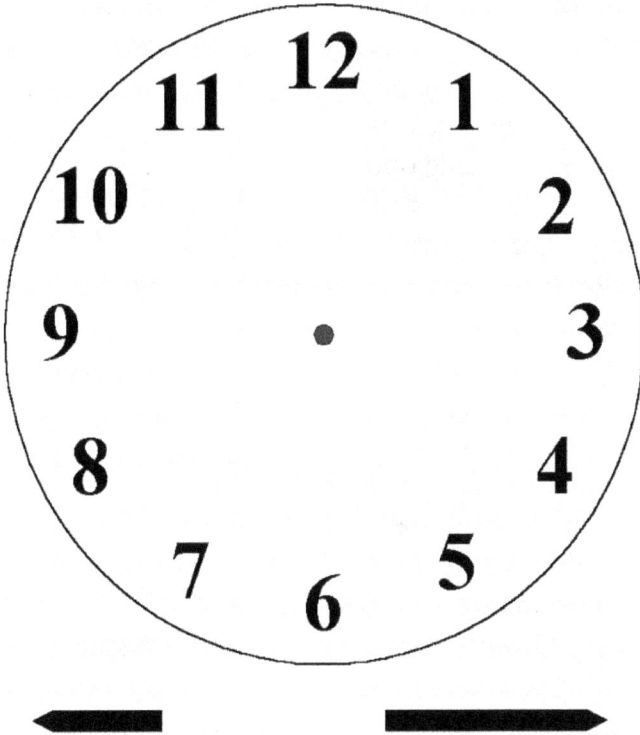

Http://www.printfree.com

## TIP SHEET: 37 INNOVATIVE STRATEGIC OPTIONS

**Here's a list of 37 Innovative Strategic Options to get you started** (some of these already appear in the 48 Smart Ways, but are equally valid for application here):

This list is designed to help you, and your team, explore possibilities. Do not discard any option that at first glance may seem to not fit your product or service; instead, try to find a practical way to apply it to your specific situation. By so doing, you challenge your creative talent and also increase the chances of coming up with truly new and innovative approaches.

1. Create new applications for existing products
2. Segment existing markets by customer types, demographics, location, buying patterns, income groups, lifestyles, purchasing preferences, etc.
3. Create new pricing options
4. Change the markets perception of your product's use
5. Change your approach to existing markets
6. Develop new channels and outlets for existing products
7. Reposition existing products
8. Create new brands
9. Fragment existing products, clients, markets
10. Bundle products and services
11. Unbundle current product offerings
12. Create add-ons to existing products and services
13. Build information and knowledge into products
14. Turn information into new products
15. Develop "downstream" products and versions
16. Develop "downstream" sales and aftermarkets
17. Introduce special services add-ons to products
18. Introduce products as add-ons to services
19. Bring new technology to existing products and services
20. Create entrepreneurs (franchises, licensees) to sell existing products and services
21. Sell technology as well as products and services (licensing)
22. Piggyback products and services with other products and services
23. Piggyback products and services with those of other companies
24. Combine two existing products into a third one
25. Enter into alliances with companies whose products, services, markets, clients, distribution channels, or outlets, complement yours
26. Buy into markets, products, services, technology, and clients through M&A 's

27. Offer a wider variety of products and services
28. Target specific pieces of competitor business
29. License brand names, logos, technology, and processes
30. Sell marketing know-how
31. Load up production and then start upgrading customers
32. Create new customers through financing
33. Develop seasonal products
34. Tie products to themes and events
35. Private labels: offer your products to others to sell under their own brand name
36. Sell what your product does, rather than the product itself
37. Differentiate your product through value-adding strategies

*Question. How do you intend to use the above list? If you don't, you will miss out on some important possibilities that could create sustainable profits!*

**Focus on growing revenues faster than costs and expenses.**

Given what we said above, this is a priority. Unexpected negatives always lurk in the background. New competitors, changing government regulations, technological innovations, sudden shifts in demand; any one of these can impact revenue generation negatively. **A company must always strive to grow faster than the overall market and the economy.**

Equally, unexpected changes in costs and expenses can happen at any time: cost of living increases, higher labor costs, rising energy prices, increased raw material costs. Any one of these can squeeze margins into non-existence. A company must always try to spend less than it can afford. Largesse and generosity based on false spending capability assumptions have bankrupted many a company, except for those bailed out by the government.

Imagine a couple trying to live on a fixed income; no matter how well they budget their expenses there will always be unexpected expenses. In addition, it is likely that while their needs will grow and prices will go up, they might survive for a while but, inevitably, their standard of living will suffer.

Companies can't live on a fixed income either. They can't save themselves into Sustained Profit. They must constantly increase their revenues at a rate greater than the growth of their costs and expenses.

Costs and expenses grow easily. If you do nothing about them, they will eat away at Profit. While companies must always work at lowering costs and expenses, that alone won't make them profitable. **They must grow their revenues.**

No matter how good companies may be at controlling costs, they can't save themselves into increased revenues. Companies that focus excessively on saving, tend to starve growth by not applying resources to opportunities. They avoid and delay critical capital and operating investments waiting for the right opportunity. Right opportunities don't just come along. They have to be created. Profit begins with revenues; there is no growth without them.

Increasing revenues can be hard to do. It takes enormous effort, money, and time to make revenues grow. Revenues are like air. You can hold your breath until you die but, to survive you must breathe. You need to keep life-giving air coming in.

During the peak of the re-engineering frenzy, many companies became so inward-focused that they literally ignored the marketplace. Before long, they began to feel the effect of reduced or inadequate revenues. Some of them never recovered from their loss of market position.

## PROTECT THE CONTINUITY OF YOUR REVENUE STREAMS TO MAINTAIN SUSTAINABILITY

At the beginning of every year, most companies have to go out into the marketplace and create their revenue streams all over again. There is no guarantee that last years' customers will buy again this year or that they will buy as much. In fact, there is a greater probability that the company will lose some customers it didn't expect to.

When companies neglect to protect their revenue streams, they expose themselves to a great vulnerability. Re-inventing the wheel by having to go out and secure a customer base every year is not smart.

The best way to ensure continuity of revenue streams is to give your customers reasons for wanting to continue doing business with you. It means shifting your emphasis from increasing sales every year to increasing and retaining customers.

Beyond that, *it also means increasing Share of Current Customers.* The quickest way to raise your sales ten percent is to sell ten percent more to your current customers.

This means moving away from wanting to sell to everybody, to selling only to those customers who are profitable and have growth potential. It means putting all your eggs in fewer, bigger, better baskets, and watching over those baskets very carefully.

It means investing time, money, and effort in finding, getting, holding and growing better, more profitable customers, establishing long-term relationships with them, and making it worthwhile for them to continue doing business with you. When you develop long-term relationships with good customers, you protect your revenue streams and make it easier to maintain your profits.

## BE GOOD AT EVERYTHING, BUT EXCEL AT
### WHAT YOUR CUSTOMERS WANT MOST

What they want today, not what they wanted a week or a month ago, or what they really don't care about.

No one can excel at everything but all of us can be better at just one thing. In todays frenzied competitive markets, however, that one thing better be something that buyers care about. It can be speed, convenience, price, or any one of a number of other qualities. Identify what your customers want most, and become the best at supplying it.

We have choices. We can be the low-cost producer that enables us to offer price advantages to customers. In every market, there is room for the low-cost producer because there are always buyers who want the least expensive product. But consumers must see the product as offering value. When a low-cost product provides reasonable quality, it is likely to be perceived as good value. If it does not, then it is perceived as cheap.

Japanese autos originally were lower priced in the U.S. market, but were perceived as low quality. As they built a reputation for good products and superior support service, demand grew and Japanese manufacturers were able to raise the prices on their autos. Today, Korean autos are going through the same the process, trying to earn a quality and reliability reputation.

Another choice is to offer the best product. If it is perceived as such (which is not always guaranteed), and customers care about best in quality or performance, then they will buy it and be willing to pay more for it. For example, studies indicate that those companies whose products are perceived as being of higher quality generate higher profits.

The reputation of quality and distinction often supports inordinately high prices: Rolls Royce, Ferrari, Bentley, and so on. A brand name equated as "best in its class" has tremendous drawing power and can carry a product line for years.

The message is that companies that identify the benefits their customers want most and create offerings that are perceived by customers as good value, are consistently most profitable.

One caveat: it is not enough to be best at something if you are not good at all the other things that make up customer expectations. The history of failures is full of companies and products that excelled at one thing but could not satisfy the composite of all the other expectations customarily associated with that product or service.

The demise of Webvan was an example of single area excellence unsupported by basic competence. The company offered a good value proposition to its customers: order your groceries via the Internet, and they will be delivered directly to your home for a small fee. The offer was excellent but the company couldn't keep up with basic logistics of food delivery, then filed for bankruptcy. In the twenty first century, excellence in **execution** of the offering is a *business survival must*. Since then other companies like Peapod have moved into the market segment, then are being displaced by grocery stores and Amazon delivering food. A single area of competence may prosper only until others pick up that same competence.

## IF YOU CAN'T BE NUMBER ONE IN YOUR CATEGORY— CREATE A NEW ONE

*And be the best at it!* If you can't win, change the game and make it even better. Most product categories already have too many suppliers competing for the top positions in today markets.

Only one product can be number one, and only a few may compete for second place. Beyond that, all others are viewed as "also-rans" Markets reward leaders; also-rans seldom generate enough profits to survive.

Understanding customers and their needs is essential to achieving Sustainable Profit Growth. Identifying unsatisfied needs is the key to creating new categories.

Back during the 50's, all cough medicines were pretty much the same: dark-colored, bad-tasting syrups. Children, who seem to have the most colds, hated the taste of the cough remedies. Getting them to take their medicine was always a major battle for parents. Then one company came up with the idea of offering fruit-flavored syrups. They were an instant hit and, for a while, that company commanded a leading position in the market.

Unfortunately, flavoring is an easily replicated feature. Soon, all brands of cough syrups were flavored. The flavor race was over. The next race involved expectorants and cough suppressants. When that race had run its course, the emphasis shifted to hours of relief: at first four, then six, then 12, and so on. After that came decongestants and another race ensued.

Finally, one company, Vicks, studied cold sufferers. They discovered that the most uncomfortable time for people with colds was at night when the symptoms kept them from sleeping. Here was a group of sufferers with a clearly unsatisfied need: relief at night. The company created a new category and a product to serve it, Nyquil. To this day, Nyquil still reigns as the cough medicine queen of the night.

A new category is often a niche market. Once identified, the strategy must be to quickly fill the need with a well-designed product and become the leader of that niche.

## Sell offerings, not products.

People don't buy products; they buy what they think the products will do for them. They buy expectations that the products will satisfy specific needs and wants. Create and sell offerings that promise (and will be perceived as) high value satisfaction.

Even today, most companies in the United States are product feature oriented. They think that their mission is to generate products. The truth is that most people don't care who makes the product or where it comes from, just as long as it does what they expect from it.

The impact of this fact should be that companies focus on crafting customer satisfaction first and products second. It also means that whatever it takes to generate that satisfaction can come from any number of sources that may, or may not, include the company's own facilities.

Product-oriented companies should learn from the travel industry where package deals are commonly offered to satisfy customer needs. Instead of forcing the customer to deal first with airlines, then hotels, then tour companies, restaurants, and so on, the travel industry offers an all-encompassing package that includes all of the above for a competitive price.

Genera Electrics Jet Engine Division has traditionally sold the obvious jet engines, plus service, plus parts, etc. Airplane manufacturers and airlines are not really interested in owning jet engines and all the paraphernalia and activities that go with them; all they really want is sustainable, reliable, thrust that will keep their planes flying safely and at a reasonable cost. The result? General Electric now sells their customers thrust. GE takes care of engines, their maintenance, and everything else, and just charges customers for what they want—thrust.

*Don't sell what you make. Sell what customers want!*

## PROVIDE VALUE BEYOND YOUR PRODUCT

Does your product take care of all your customers' needs? Is the performance of your product so superior that competitors can't match it? Is your price so low that competitors can't equal it? Is product all that your customers want or need?

Companies are discovering that customers want and need more than just product. Of course, service is a well-recognized need but it has become a given. Everyone provides service (or claims to), and if you don't you are not in the game.

What is there beyond product, service, and price then? The answer is -- helping customers fulfill the mission for which they buy the product or service. For example, why do companies buy raw materials or product components? The immediate answer is to produce their own products. If all you do is help them achieve that immediate need, you are a competent supplier, but not a great one, and probably not one that customers want to partner with over the long-term.

Helping customers achieve the immediate purpose of their purchase may get you in the door, *but it doesn't guarantee you'll be around for the long haul.* You need to get beyond the immediate purpose of the purchase to your customers ultimate mission. That mission is to provide superior satisfactions to their customers and, in so doing, to generate profitable growth for their own business.

If you sell to businesses and want customers to partner with you long-term, you must help them increase their revenues and profits better than your competitors do. You can't do this on product performance and price alone. You must learn how to bring to bear all the resources of your organization to help your customers improve their revenues and lower their costs, thus enhancing their growth and Profit. In other words, *help your customers be better at their business, and you will become better at yours.*

## DISCRIMINATE IN FAVOR OF PROFITABLE CUSTOMERS WHEN PROVIDING BENEFITS

*When you provide all your customers, good and bad, with the same benefits, you are penalizing promising customers, and wasting valuable resources on unpromising ones.*

No company in the world, no matter how large, has enough resources to waste on unproductive, unpromising, and unprofitable customers. Consider your market a garden; would you waste scarce water on weeds?

Good customers will stay with you in good and bad times. They will focus more on value than price. Bad customers will demand as much or more than good ones, and will drop you as soon as someone comes along with a lower price. There is no future in rewarding bad customers with good resources. Make your profitable customers special and let them know it.

## ANALYZE PROFIT BY ACCOUNT

A recent study indicated that a large percentage of U.S. companies do not track Profit by Account. As a result, it is believed that many companies may have as much as fifty percent unprofitable customers! This means that they must be devoting an inordinately large percentage of their resources to unpromising, unrewarding accounts.

Quite often, your biggest customer can be your least profitable one. Companies that buy in large quantities will often drive a hard bargain when it comes to prices. Despite this, their suppliers find them attractive as customers because of the sales volume they offer. In time, suppliers find themselves devoting more and more resources to supporting these low-or-no-profit customers. They can't improve their margins, but on the other hand, they can't reduce their support without running the risk of losing the business. High volume, low profit customers are appreciated because they pay the rent and keep the plant running. At that point, the supplier may be in business only to keep the plant running.

Know who your profitable customers are. Then, concentrate on making them more profitable and you will be profitable too.

## GRATITUDE GENERATES PROFITS

*No matter what business you're in—you are in the relationship business, and an important part of any relationship is gratitude.* Gratitude is an uncommon virtue in marketing. As a result, most customers feel unappreciated. Gratitude can be a great way of differentiating your company from competitors.

Gratitude can start as early as the inquiry stage. When prospects request information, obviously, we should do our utmost to answer all possible questions. But, why not?

- Also show class by thanking prospects for contacting us.
- Create a sense of inevitability by also telling them that we look forward to doing business with them.
- Take it even further by offering a reward for having contacted us.
- Thank customers for becoming our friends when inquiries become sales.
- Stay in touch with them, when they have become our friends, in as many ways as possible and offer them special benefits as friends.

*Remember, friends are people we choose to treat in special ways. Turn sales into customers, and customers into friends, and sustainable profits will follow.*

## PURGE YOUR PRODUCT LINES PERIODICALLY

No company can afford to carry unprofitable products. No company can afford to carry a full product line to please every type of customer; it just isn't profitable. *Products must earn their keep.* Track the Profit of all products on a regular basis. Those that don't provide enough revenue, growth, or margin should become candidates for elimination.

When we don't get rid of unproductive products, we waste resources we could be applying to products that do generate revenues and good margins.

Granted, there may be products that are not particularly profitable that customers still want us to keep in our lines. In these cases, we must find ways to make them more profitable by either raising their price or by lowering their cost. Get rid of losers; they increase your inventory, chew up working capital, and distract sales efforts from your winners. They kill your profits.

## DESIGN YOUR PRODUCT MIX FOR HIGHER PROFIT

Your best-selling products may not be the most profitable. Sustainable gross profit is made up of products with different profit margins. Usually, some products have higher volume but lower margins, and others higher margins but lower volumes. In the end, what counts is the sustainable gross profit. How a company arrives at its sustainable gross profit is a mix of high volume/low margin, and high margin/low volume products. Designing and promoting that mix is critical to Profit.

Another way of looking at margin mix is to say:

- High volume low margin products pay the rent.
- Low volume high margin products generate the profits.

Quite often, companies sell too many low margin products, usually because they may have a lower price and are easier to sell, and not enough high margin product for just the opposite reason, that is, higher price and harder to sell. The danger can be that it may take as much or more resources to manufacture and sell low margin products. Margin mix must be analyzed constantly to protect Profit, but also to spot trends.

*Occasionally, slower moving products start selling faster. This could indicate that customers have found a new use for it that offers the possibility of developing a completely new niche.*

*Conversely, fast selling products could begin to slow down. This could indicate that they may be reaching the end of their life cycle.*

No company can afford to ignore either trend.

*Define your target sustainable gross profit and design your product mix accordingly.*

## GIVE EVERY CUSTOMER A CHANCE TO UPGRADE

Once customers buy your product and, assuming they were satisfied with it, why not give them a chance to achieve even greater satisfaction with an upgrade? We should all learn from the software companies who do this all the time.

In any given product-line there will a variety of offerings from low price to high. If the line is properly designed, most customers will opt for middle range products. After they have experienced satisfaction with that level product, they may be ready to consider the next level up. Why not offer it to them? Most companies miss out on the opportunity to up sell their existing customers.

Provide your customers with a variety of good value options that will increase their satisfaction and, in so doing, improve your sustainable gross profit.

## REVIEW YOUR PRICING FREQUENTLY

*Every day that you keep your prices below what they should be is a day's profit lost. Conversely, every day you keep your prices above where they ought to be is a days' sales lost.* Be careful, however, to not confuse or irritate your customers by raising and lowering your prices too often. The end result will be a loss of credibility as is the case with airlines and oil companies.

Most companies are too slow to modify their prices, and too timid when they do. Businesses should constantly be testing the pricing limits of their products and services. Occasionally, a price may go too high and sales may begin to suffer. So, *lower your price!* There's nothing wrong with changing your mind or prices.

Service businesses and professional firms tend to underprice their services. They seem to think that what they do can easily be replicated by others at lower prices. If the business is an easy access, that is, one that can be set up with little or no investment, they may be right. Novices can underestimate the value and cost of the work involved, and thus lower their prices unrealistically or even unprofitably. But the fact that they are novices and untested may act against them by detracting from their credibility.

*The flip side of this is that sometimes raising your price increases your credibility.*

In every business, there will always be some fool who lowers prices too far and another one who buys from him. The same could probably be said for those who overprice their services.

## SELL VALUE, NOT PRICE

Why do customers buy your product? They do so because they perceive value in the product and its price. You need to know what value they perceive and price accordingly. You also need the value message in all your communications with customers.

Every contact with customers and prospects must constantly

remind them of the value that your product delivers. *The value message should be so powerful that price considerations lose their importance.* When you sell on price, you have no position with your customers. There is no reason for them to stay with you. Any competitor willing to sell cheaper can take them away

## Make selling a Ministry of Service

The word 'Sell' comes from the Norwegian word 'Selje' which means To Serve. When you sell with a spirit of service, you are ministering to your customer's needs. *Selling is not about you, your company, or your product; it's about the customer.* Your job is to understand as much as about that customer that you become an invaluable adviser. No matter what business you are in, you should be in the business of making people lives better. When you have this focus, you will distinguish yourself, your company, and your product from all your competitors who are only selling widgets. Customers are constantly bombarded by people who are in the widget-selling business. When they run into someone who is in the life-improvement business, they can't help but notice, appreciate, and reward the difference.

## Redesign your business

The design of a business is the way it creates and delivers satisfaction to customers. Your business design is like the design of a car. The car you drove 20 years ago would probably not meet your needs today. What model year is your business design? Has it been updated to satisfy todays more demanding customers?

Consider your business design a system that:

- Finds customers
- Identifies their needs
- Creates a means of satisfying those needs, and

- Develops an effective delivery system that ensures that satisfaction.

It takes time to develop a business design that consistently accomplishes this goal in a profitable way. Some companies never do.

The problem is that most business designs tend to lose their effectiveness over time because they don't adapt to changing customer priorities. Customers change. Values tend to change with each generation. They change according to economic cycles. Priorities evolve as lifestyles change, and as customers aspirations and preferences change. These constantly moving factors make business designs obsolete.

*Yesterday's customer perception of value may not be the same as todays, and today's values may not be the same as tomorrows.*

People lives are more hectic, more time-pressured today than at any time in the past. Everybody is multi-tasking just trying to keep up. Fewer people have time for leisurely shopping; some don't have time for any shopping at all. Most of today's business designs were created at an earlier time for customers who lived differently than they do today. The Internet has created a completely new dimension in the way people communicate, do business, and obtain information. Yet, many businesses still don't recognize that increasing numbers of customers are surfing the internet to shorten the information gathering needed to make their purchases, especially those that are more significant.

When our customer's lives and priorities change, so must the ways we seek to satisfy their needs. We must change our business design to preserve our customers and protect our profits.

Customers also expect their suppliers to use the best technology to constantly provide them with improved products and services. A frequent problem, however, is that suppliers fall in love with the technology without finding the equivalent value for the customer. Having the best technology does not automatically make a product or a company better. The winners in the marketplace are those who have the best technology with the best applications.

*Question. How often do you purge your product lines? If you don't, you are probably harboring some losers that cost you money instead of producing it.*

# CHAPTER SIX
# Differentiate: Create Powerful Perceptions!

**Question:** How do you differentiate your products, company, and yourself from all others?

**Answer:** Make sure no one will ever confuse your offerings with those of your competitors.

## WHY DIFFERENTIATE?

When the famous author Oscar Wilde spoke at an Ivy League college, all the students showed up wearing a lily in their lapels, something Wilde was known for. Acknowledging the gesture, he said, *"Imitation is the sincerest form of flattery."*

In business, imitation is not the sincerest form of flattery but the quickest form of competition creation. It has a disadvantage that it is "me too-ism" at its worst! In business, *uniqueness is valued highly*; imitation is definitely less so. In today's fast-paced marketplace, advanced technology has helped manufacturers generate products of such high quality that they have created a problem for their customers -- and themselves.

## COMMODITIZATION!

Commoditization means competitive products are so equally good that, to the customer, they all look alike. Several things happen when customers cannot distinguish between products:

- Brands lose their importance.
- Loyalty disappears.
- Price becomes the main factor in decision making.

- Sales decrease.
- Margins drop.
- Market shares shrink.
- Advertising becomes useless
- Profits shrink

## PERCEPTION, POWER AND PROFIT

In the marketplace, perception is so powerful that it has an enormous impact on profit. When you think profit, be sure to think about the perception you wish the customers to have regarding *your company, your brand and your products*. Rather than leave perception to chance, why not design it yourself and reinforce it at every customer contact point?

Perception is what we think reality is; however, the two don't always match. A football team may perceive itself to be the best and find out the hard reality on the field when it meets a better competitor. On the other hand, a team may perceive the opposing team to be overwhelmingly powerful, and find out on the field that the opposition's players are just humans like everyone else, and actually beat them.

Perceptions dominate the marketplace. Reality rarely wins. If reality were the stronger of the two then - by that logic - the best quality product would be the best seller in every market. That is not the case. Quite often, the best-selling products in any market are just mediocre...less qualified. Yes, it is unfair, but true.

Products may dominate the market because of advertising, brand name recognition, superior distribution, predatory pricing, or simply because they offer the average consumer a better deal for the price.

## PERCEPTION AND ENTERTAINMENT

Perception is evident as a force in every market. Take entertainment for example. In the early days of radio there was a popular singer, a "crooner" as they called them then, by the name of Russ Columbo. General consensus had it that he was the best singer on the air. Nevertheless, Bing Crosby, an excellent singer, but not as good as Columbo, made the big time.

Later, Frank Sinatra came along, and ran away with a new generation of fans. Sinatra was a good singer, maybe even a great one at certain points in his career. In his later years, however, the voice was long gone, and his renditions were not of the quality his early ones had been. Yet, he dominated the market for many years despite the existence of many good singers who just were never able to create his kind of brand equity. *Perception overwhelmed reality.*

In today's run-away, look-alike, advertising-filled marketplace, creating a distinctive perception for a product, service, company, or person is becoming increasingly difficult. *Differentiation has never been more important, yet harder to achieve. But, when you do, it is profit power.*

Today' customers are plagued with endless messages and offers from an equally endless number of suppliers. End result? Confused customers who see all products as equal, endless clones with no distinguishing virtues. When all products look alike, they are perceived as commodities. When that happens, the only distinguishing feature is price, which means low prices and poor profits.

What Is left? In the age of commoditization, how do you make your product, your brand, your company, and your offerings distinctive? Product features by themselves won't do it. Why? Because they don't necessarily represent value to the customer. All too often, in their quest for differentiation, companies come up with features that are meaningless to customers.

## SHELL OIL AND PERCEPTION

Years ago, Shell Oil Company promoted its supposedly special additive Shell X100 as an ingredient that made its product superior. To Shells credit, X100's benefits were listed, but were perceived as adding any value. To be effective, a differentiator must be perceived as valuable by the customer. It must offer a valued benefit.

Differentiation must be based on something that is important to the buyer. The product itself is rarely important, but what it does for the buyer is. Even more important is what the buyer *perceives* as valuable. Differentiation is a product of perception. For example, look at Intel's strategy. "Intel-inside" might have seemed a waste of money since consumers buy computers, not chips. But the reason why the slogan worked was because Intel's products are *perceived* as more reliable, and reliability is important to consumers who purchase PCs.

## PERCEPTION AND APPLE

In today's world of look-alike products, design can often be a differentiator. Apple Computer was able to revive wilting sales by offering daring designs. They really didn't do that much for consumers, other than brighten up their desks. When compared to the drab, mundane designs of all other computers, Apple's products did appeal to those who wanted something brighter and distinctive.

## PERCEPTION AND BMW

When auto manufacturers were trying to top one another with new looks and a plethora of features. BMW came up with a powerful slogan *"The ultimate driving experience."* To those who wanted performance and excitement, "the ultimate driving experience" was worth paying more for.

What counts with consumers isn't the product as much as their experience with it. Study each stage of the customers' contact with your product, from the moment of awareness of its existence to the moment of its disposal. Then ask yourself, what can I do at this stage that would be of special value to the customer and would be different from what all others offer? Study what everybody else does, then do something different and ask yourself the question customers are bound to ask about that difference "Who cares?" *Unless the difference has value for customers, they won't care.* When customers see you doing what everybody else does, you look like everybody else, and it becomes harder to make a profit.

## COMPETING THROUGH DIFFERENTIATION

"I've got a lovely bunch of coconuts" says the old song. But if you really had a bunch of coconuts, how would you price them? Would you price them all the same because "coconuts is coconuts?" Or would you price some higher than others? And if you did price some higher, what basis would you use to justify doing so? *Size, perhaps? Weight? Color?*

To most customers all coconuts look alike. When items look alike, how do the customers make the buying decision? Usually on price, that's how. The lowest price wins. The rationale is, if all products look alike, then they must be the same and, if they are, then why pay more for one versus another?

If the prices are related to size, then the customers' question will be, why does size affect the price? If bigger relates to the taste and quality of the coconut, then customer may see a relationship between size, price, and value. It all comes down to this:

*Look-alike products confuse the customer and diminish the perception of value.*

## WHAT MAKES ONE PRODUCT DIFFERENT FROM OTHERS?

When considering what would be the best way to differentiate your product from others, first you need to ask, what would the customer view as the "Next Best Alternative" to your product? Whatever it is, that is what you must surpass and differentiate from.

As for how will your product differentiate itself, there are the following areas to explore:

- **Brand.** Is your brand more powerful? Is it viewed as premium?
- **Service.** What is special and better about your service that differentiates it in the market?
- **Features and Benefits.** Which features of your product offer greater benefits from the point of view of the customers?
- **Quality.** Is your product's quality demonstrably better than the competition in ways that customers appreciate and value?
- **Design and Style.** Is your product more attractive? Is it perceived as stylish?
- **Easily Accessible?** Is it easy to purchase?

## FINDING MEANINGFUL DIFFERENTIATION

It is easy to be different, however, it is hard to be meaningfully different. Anyone can be different; all they need to do is paint themselves green, or some other color. (I don't care what Kermit the Frog says. Being green *is* easy. Besides, in his case he had no choice.) The point is - so what? Why should that be of any value to the customer?

- The difference needs to relate to something that has meaning for the customer; otherwise, it's just a useless add-on. An interesting example of someone who has made a color difference meaningful is Michael Scott Karpovich, the motivational speaker. Michael's message has to do with making adversity work to your advantage. His trademark is sneakers of two different colors, one red, the other lavender. What does this have to do with his message? Michael tells the story of his youth, of his being brain damaged, and having to cope with being different. Being dyslexic, he says he also had difficulty distinguishing right from left. But Michael found a solution: he wears the red shoe on his right foot because it reminds him that it is on the right (Red and Right both begin with R), and the lavender one on the left foot following the same logic. Is it true? It doesn't matter; it works. Michael uses this rationale to move onto many other ways of turning adversity into advantage. It is a charming and very effective way of being different. The positioning of the different colored shoes per se is meaningless, but the lesson learned is the perception and where the clients find value.

- After years of trying to "grow up" through a variety of car models, Volkswagen finally woke up to the value of its Beetle and brought it back! It was different. It was cute. And it was selling like hotcakes. Was it functional? Was it high-tech? Was it light-years ahead of the competition in technological innovation? No, but who cares? It worked. Despite, the durability of the Beetle image, Volkswagen has again decided to discontinue it. Will that be a good decision in a time when mileage and price have become so important? It remains to be seen.

Almost all successful cases of differentiation have worked because they found something that related to what customers value in some way. Were these cases always the product of careful analysis? No, many of them were sheer dumb luck! But who cares? It worked! What this does tell us, however, is that intuition can work as well as or better than analysis. It can also fail. But then, so can analysis.

- In ancient Greece, when people entered the temple of the Oracle of Delphi (famous for "on- target" predictions), the first inscription they found on the wall was "Know thyself!" In today's temple of market predictions, the inscription would say, "Know thy customer!" The lesson here is that the more we know our customer, whether intuitively or analytically, the more likely we are to find an area of value that will allow us to identify a meaningful differentiation.

**Point.** Customers must perceive your differences in products as worthwhile. **Benefits increase the importance of price!** Worthwhile benefits that relate to customers' needs or wants offer value; therefore,

- Value justifies price.
- Value makes buying decisions easier.

**Perceived value is the key to your profit.**

The product could be different, but if the difference is meaningless to the customer then it represents no value. The more you differentiate your product in ways that are beneficial to the customer, the more value it will represent, and the more you can raise your price.

**The question now becomes – How Can We Create Valuable Differences in Our Products?**

First, we must find out what is important to the customer. What does the customer value? How can we find this? The most common sources of information regarding customer preferences are surveys and focus panels. Both have their advantages and their detractors.

Surveys pose questions regarding buying habits. Customers supposedly provide honest answers. Unfortunately, people often don't know what they like, or why they like it. In addition, when they have no answer, they may invent one.

Focus panels gather a group of people in the same room where an experienced moderator asks them questions about their preferences. A problem that appears with focus panels is that personalities can influence the opinions of the participants and weaken the validity of the outcome.

## ANALYZE CUSTOMER'S BUYING PROCESS

Another approach is to record the customer's reactions to each stage of the acquisition or buying process. It starts by dividing the acquisition process into stages. Let's use furniture buying as an example.

- What's the first step? Perhaps it is the awareness of the need or desire to acquire furniture. What triggers the desire to buy new furniture? Starting a household? Moving to a new home? Remodeling? Damage to existing furniture?
- What are the emotions associated with this stage? Excitement? Delight? Anticipation? Fun? Dread? Boredom? Having identified the emotions, we must ask ourselves what can we do to improve the customer's experience? What can we do to differentiate our product at this stage of the process? What can we do to enhance the awareness stage?
- Having identified the emotions, we must ask ourselves what can we do to improve the customer's experience? What can we do to differentiate our product at this stage of the process? What can we do to enhance the customer's experience during the awareness stage that will also differentiate our product?
- What's the next step in the buying process? It could be developing more information about the product and exploring diverse options. How does the customer go about getting information about furniture? Internet? Mailer Ads? Newspapers? Radio? TV? Referrals? Personal experience? Store window displays?
- What are the customer's emotions in this stage? Surprise? Excitement? Frustration? Sticker shock? Confusion?
- How can we supply information to the customer that is genuinely practical? What can we do differently from our competitors? How can we simplify the information gathering

and speed up the buying process? How can we make the information stage less painful, less time consuming, and more rewarding?

- What would be the next step? It could be the customer's first contact with the potential supplier. How would that contact be made? By telephone? Internet? Personal visit to the store? What are the customer's emotions during this stage? Uncertainty? Surprisingly pleasant, or just plain fatiguing? Irritation?

- How can we make this experience more satisfying and helpful to the customer? What could we do that would really differentiate us from all the other suppliers and build a relationship with the customer?

Good Questions!

**Let's check the sequence of steps that might involve purchasing furniture. Customer Purchase Steps.**

When you think through the 11-step process that customers go through as they make an in-person purchase, ask yourself what could be done to make each step a better, more distinctive experience.

1. **Awareness.** The customer identifies a need.
2. **Education.** The customer searches for information that will improve his or her knowledge about the product and the offerings in the marketplace.
3. **Contact.** The customer telephones, e-mails, or visits retailers.
4. **Selection.** Customer selects certain piece or pieces of furniture at a specific retailer.
5. **Negotiation.** Customer and supplier seek mutually acceptable price and terms
6. **Acquisition.** The customer makes the buying decision.
7. **Delivery.** Furniture is delivered to the customer.

8. **Follow up.** Supplier checks customer satisfaction.
9. **Relationship.** Supplier stays in touch with customer.
10. **Repeat sale.** Customer returns to retailer for next purchase.
11. **Disposal.** Retailer helps customer dispose of old furniture.

Each of these steps offers opportunities for differentiation by increasing customer satisfaction. For example, in the awareness stage we might slant our advertising toward the satisfaction of redecorating the home with new furniture. We could make customers more aware of how furniture ages without our even noticing it. We could make customers aware of how much fashion has changed in furniture.

In the education stage we could invite customers to seminars that would show them how to decorate their home and emphasize how they could budget for new furniture. And so on.

You can begin to see how this method of exploring the customer's experience and emotions in each stage, all the way from awareness to purchasing to delivery, and even to disposal of the furniture sometime in the future, can reveal numerous opportunities for creating valuable benefits for the customer. At the same time that we are creating these benefits we should also be exploring how we can use them to differentiate ourselves from the competition.

Coconuts, furniture, cars, professional services, you name it. Just about anything and everything in today's marketplace is facing commoditization. For the first time in human history supply exceeds demand. Consumers are bombarded with endless information (and disinformation) to the point where they tune out practically every commercial message.

At the same time, manufacturers have improved their processes to the point that product quality has become a given. Advertising tries hard to make products distinguishable almost to the point that you can no longer tell what it is that they're advertising.

Everything seems to look like everything else. In the midst of all this confusion, how is a customer supposed to make a good buying decision? If the customer decides that price is the only differentiating factor, then the product with the lowest price will be selected.

*Unfortunately, customers are often unaware that BEHIND EVERY LOW PRICE THERE IS A HIDDEN COST!*

When, as a customer, you see a low price you must ask yourself what is the seller removing that allows him to still make a profit?

Customers may think they are getting the same product at the lower price, but the reality could turn out to be different.

What's the answer?

*Create distinctive offerings with benefits that customers perceive as superior value. Then align your prices with the perceived higher value and you will benefit from increased profits.*

## TO BE OR NOT TO BE

Life is full of choices. Unfortunately, too many for most of us to make good choices every time. Because there are so many choices, the hardest thing about making one is deciding what the product **should not** to be or do. But that is the most important decision we need to make. Once we weed out the inappropriate, the inadequate, and the downright silly, our differentiation decision-making process becomes simpler.

So, what should the product **not** be?

- Let's start with *irrelevant*. If the customer could care less about the difference we are considering, we should drop it ~ fast! It is important to be pitiless in this process of weeding out options. We don't have the time or the resources to explore every interesting avenue.
- What else? We must avoid *confusing* "clever" with "meaningful." Clever differences might appeal to our sense of intellectual sophistication. Very few truly clever differences have enough meaning to customers that it will change their buying decision.

- Another type of differentiation that seldom works is *subtle*. Mr. and Mrs. Average Consumers are anything but subtle. If you don't believe it, just check the most popular sitcoms on television. You can see the punch lines coming from a mile away.
- *Trendy* is another type of differentiation that should probably be avoided. Although they may offer short-term possibilities, trendy differentiations tend to fade quickly. It may be possible to constantly create trendy differentiations and capitalize on them while they're hot. The problem is they will likely become passé before they can be fully developed and you see a ROI.
- "Taste" as a differentiator needs to be examined with care. Although the famous writer H.L. Mencken said, "*No one ever went broke underestimating the American public's taste.*" Attempting differentiation through anything that could be perceived as being in bad taste is very risky.

## EXERCISE: DEFINING DIFFERENTIATION CRITERIA

How do you want your product, company, or self to be perceived? This may be hard to define. Try making a list of adjectives that describe the impression you are searching for. For example, *what words would you use to describe a product that you plan to target at upscale consumers such as mid-career executives with major corporations?*

**Assume it is an especially designed attaché case that offers a built-in flexible computer and monitor, a detachable smart phone, and Wi-Fi.**

What thoughts and feelings would you want to inspire?

Think of the problems it solves for executives who are on the go most of the time. What does it mean for the busy person who can't afford to be tied to a desk, a desktop computer, or a regular telephone?

What differentiating words come to mind to describe how the busy owner of such an attaché case would feel? Below are several words that might apply; please feel free to change them if you prefer other descriptive words.

On the line next to the words write the thoughts and emotions that are inspired by each one.

(*Suggestion: bring in other people to help you generate ideas. Remember: two or more minds are better than one – as long as they are not on the same pair of shoulders.*)

- Free? (Example: Really? How much will I save? Is there a catch?)
- Unencumbered?
- Connected?
- Self-sufficient?
- At ease?
- Unworried?
- Unhurried?
- In charge?
- In touch?
- Hands-on?
- In control?
- Powerful?

Association of Ideas:

Now, use the thoughts you included on the lines next to the above words, and use them to answer the following questions while trying to create valuable differentiation in each one.

- What images do these words evoke?
- What symbols would best represent them?
- What would you call such a product?
- What should it look like?

- What kind of person would you expect to see carrying it?
- What name would you give it?
- Why would anyone buy it?
- Where would you sell it?
- What services would you bundle with it?
- What "downstream" items would you offer?
- What would you include in a product line?

Let's keep these thoughts on tap for when we get to the section on differentiating your product. At this point we have plenty of input to help us set the criteria for differentiating this product. We know the following things:

- We want the product to be perceived as the kind of management tool high-powered executives would normally use.
- It must be associated with independence, freedom, control, smart, stylish, practical, and tech-savvy.

**Summary: Differentiation is the solution to the problem of Commoditization. As global competition becomes fiercer with every passing day, growth and profit will slow and become more difficult.**

Two things will be essential to surviving and thriving:

1. Differentiation
2. Innovation.

Start working on them now because it will never be too early to develop solutions that create new perceptions, products, and markets that boost growth and profit.

*Question. Do your products really distinguish themselves from those of your competition? If they don't do so in a way that generates customer perception of value, you are offering commodities and your ability to get higher profits from higher prices is substantially reduced.*

## WHICH BENEFITS DO TODAY'S CUSTOMERS VALUE?

*Are you offering your customers the same as yesterday? Then you are offering them less – and they know it.*

Customers don't buy products. They buy what they think the product can do for them. Basically, they are looking for satisfaction of a need or a want that they usually cannot define well, but they know satisfaction when they get it. Therefore, product **features** are rarely what they want. They are looking for **benefits.**

A world filled with growing wants and needs is also filled with problems and opportunities for creating new benefits in the form of products and services. The following list of key benefits is loaded with opportunities to satisfy peoples' needs and wants with new and innovative ways, products, and services.

## THE GIFT OF TIME

Time is irretrievable. People are increasingly busy with more things to take care of than ever before. As a result, their time is highly valued. Anything you can do to help them get results faster, save time, be more productive, will be appreciated. Oftentimes, they will also be willing to pay more for that benefit. What can you do to create or save more time for your customer? Can you get your product to the customer faster and better?

## EASINESS

*Make things convenient and easier for customers, and they will buy!* For example, buying online is a real convenience, but many companies have such complex and frustrating online ordering procedures that they undo the value of the benefit.

## Customer-Focused Customer Service

Almost everywhere around the world, customer service has become a joke, but an unpleasant rather than funny one. It shouldn't be hard to find out what customers want in the way of customer service. All you have to do is observe, ask, and listen. If you are having a hard time finding a good model of customer service, go to Nordstrom, and observe how they treat customers: the questions they ask, the ways they suggest solutions to customer needs, the quality of their packaging, and the very visible amount of thought they have put into designing their service and returns policy. But the most important difference in Nordstrom's customer service is that it is generated by people serving people, rather than automated procedures.

## Good Value for the Price

Do your customers feel it's worth it? Customers who feel they are getting their money's worth tend to be more loyal, less price-motivated and less inclined to defect. Customers hate to feel they have "been taken" by a supplier of products or services. Say, you bought a very nice expensive suit last week and only to find out that two days later, because of a "special" sale, you could have gotten it for far less.

*What do you think when you see something discounted 70 percent?*

- That having bought the same thing earlier at full price you were cheated?
- That the 70 percent lower price is probably closer to what it should have been?
- That the store hasn't been able to sell the product?
- That the product is obsolete or out of style?

Beware how you discount. People like to get something good for less price, but they know that really good products and services don't come cheap. Therefore, stress the value of your product or service at all times. Work value into every communication with customers. Keep in mind that value is a perception. Give careful thought to all the ways you can create that perception. Make value your alternative to price competition.

## EXPERIENCES

The only thing that counts is the Customer Experience. Buying products and services can become drudgery, boring, unexciting, work, and frustration unless we can turn that process into an exciting, stimulating experience. Most of us have a long list of things we probably should get for our home such as a new appliance, lighting fixtures, rugs, new floors, etc. A cruise may not do anything for our home, but is a lot more fun, exciting, and satisfying than a new rug. Which would you rather spend your money on?

Granted, we know we need to buy a new rug, but where is the fun in that? If you were in the rug business, how would you create customer excitement and emotion about buying a rug? Can you learn anything from the world of entertainment? If Disney sold rugs, how would they go about it?

## PRACTICAL TECHNOLOGICAL IMPROVEMENTS AND NOVELTIES

This is where innovation and technology can make a huge difference. By itself, technology is not a competitive advantage unless it does something customers value. Connectivity, supplied by cellular telephones, has become a major element of social networking. The tsunami-like growth of the cell phone industry would have slowed down to a dribble if the technology firms had limited their message to just creating a connection. But when Apple introduced the I Pod and the concept of I-Tunes, the world changed.

Then along came the I-Phone which added computer capabilities to telephone connectivity, followed by the I-Pad which, like the

Amazon Kindle, allowed users to also download and read books. Apple changed the world again and again. The value that these innovations bring is that they eliminate boredom. Technology by itself is merely tactical, but with the added value of special customer desired applications, it is a super competitive advantage.

## CUSTOMIZATION AND PERSONALIZATION

Customers are special in their perception of their needs, wants, preferences, and themselves. You walk into a store, and the clerk greets you by your name. You are now special, more than just a regular customer; you are somebody special. You drop off your car for regular maintenance at the dealership where you bought it. The service representative has a record of your purchase and your regular maintenance, they call you by your name and even though they do this for all their clients, you still feel special.

Your suit was made to order rather than just pulled off the rack, and you now feel you are in a special category. Your customers are special. You have to make them feel special by customizing and personalizing their experience.

## FREEDOM

People are imprisoned by their obligations, commitments and responsibilities. More and more they have less 'Me Time'. Parents are constantly bogged down by their children's school schedules, after school activities, medical appointments and treatments, sports, and educational needs. Those same parents must also devote time to their parents needs as they age. Of course, all of this is outside of home and work-related commitments, which can require overtime, business travel, etc. What could your product or service do to help them handle all of these chores, relieve them from the stress, or put their minds at ease? Could any of these tasks be made simpler, more efficient, or even eliminated with the use of technology?

## Quality of Life

As Boomers age and their physical limitations increase, they will have need of products and services that can make their lives more livable. What can you do with your products and services to help seniors and the disabled? What could you do to make retirement more affordable and comfortable?

## Protection

People want to be protected from harm and damage in all the aspects of their life. Personal safety and security for themselves and their loved ones is a primal need. Health and fitness are a growing concern for all generations as well. Protection of their property, their savings and investments has become a priority in light of economic volatility.

## The Five Rs

The key needs that demand benefit solutions to make life better are: **Recognition. Reinforcement. Rewards. Recreation. Relief.**

### Recognition

Millions of people around the world perform their duties day after day without ever receiving any kind of recognition. Could your company find a way to make a profit by helping to provide recognition for those who deserve it? Think how it would increase people's motivation and productivity?

### Reinforcement

Every day is filled with challenges to our confidence and self-esteem. What products and services could provide that little boost that might motivate people to overcome these challenges and keep on doing what they need to do day after day?

## Rewards

Sports are filled with trophies, medals, ribbons, titles, and so on. They are rewards for goals, touchdowns, and points that are considered worthy accomplishments. Every day people at work and at home labor to achieve goals and results that are also accomplishments, but they rarely receive rewards for them because they are considered part of the job. They have nothing to show for their achievements other than the regular pay they receive. What could you do to create a whole new industry that attends to this need?

## Recreation

In a world where work is a major part of everyday life, people increasingly look forward to vacations, entertainment, sports and fun. Not only have these interests become businesses and industries, but can be added and integrated into many products and services. Are you considering this possibility?

## Relief

The pharmaceutical and healthcare industries supposedly are in the business of providing relief for those who are sick, in pain, tired, overwhelmed, fatigued and stressed. Most people have a combination of those symptoms at the end of the normal day. TV helps relieve some but there is need for more ways of providing relief to tired people. What businesses would have the necessary elements to offer new solutions to this need?

*Question. When was the last time you met face-to-face with a customer? Even via Zoom or Skype? If you don't meet with customers* on a regular basis, it is unlikely that you understand what they want. You may assume that you know, but you probably don't.

Question. Customers change with the times. They all age, new generations show up, needs shift as incomes rise or drop, priorities evolve, new technologies create new expectations, and so on. What is the current composition of your customer base compared to five years ago?

# CHAPTER SEVEN
## The Cost of Lost Opportunity

### MYRIAD OTHER WAYS TO LOSE MONEY

There are plenty of ways for people and companies to lose money, many of which they never realize. Missing an opportunity is bad enough, but missing what it might have produced is horrifying. Sort of like missing your flight on a prepaid 2-week vacation in Europe – only a lot worse.

Picture this one. On the same day that Alexander Graham Bell turned in his application for a patent on his invention of the telephone, another inventor, Elisha Gray, turned in a very similar patent, only he did so a little later than Bell. I wonder if Elisha ever knew what the cost of that lost opportunity was.

This one could make most of us cry. Recently, a friend of mine turned in an RFP (Request for Proposal) for a deal where, if he had won – and he stood a good chance of doing so, it would have been worth $10,000,000. He waited to the last minute to fill out the forms and then sent his son to personally deliver the RFP. His son got stuck in traffic and turned in the RFP half an hour after the deadline. *Adios* $10,000,000!

As they say in the infomercials: "*But, wait!! There's more.*"

### DID YOU KNOW THAT YOU MAY BE LOSING AS MUCH AS 75% OF POTENTIAL SALES?

All companies lose potential sales for a myriad of reasons. Most often, it is because a salesperson, an executive, or some employee, just didn't do a good enough job of handling the prospects' objection to the company's price. I doubt that any company keeps track of the impact of lost sales. What they don't realize, however, is that, on an average, most salespeople lose at least 3 out of every 4 opportunities to close the sale. What that says is that the company only landed a quarter of what was possible. In other words, they are losing 75% of potential sales. *If a company makes a $20,000,000 profit, it really could have made $100,000,000 in sales– if only their salespeople had known how to beat the sales objection.*

## Do You Realize the Impact of Lost Sales Opportunities?

The impact is not only the loss of the specific sale and its revenue, *but the continuity of more sales.* When you lose customers, you lose the revenue and profit they would bring in the future. What is the average lifespan of your customer relationships? If a customer purchases your product/service once a year paying $150, and continues to do so for 20 years, the lifetime value of that customer is $3,000. If the salesperson fails to close a prospect that would purchase that amount each year, the cost of lost opportunity is $3,000. Right? Or, is it more?

**Remember: annual purchases times the number of years average customer continues to buy, equals Customer Lifetime Value. Calculate it now and make every employee aware of it!!**

## Transaction-Based Relationships Lose Money-Making Opportunities All the Time

Actually, the cost of lost opportunity is far more because a customer, if properly informed and stimulated, can buy many more products and services from you. Unfortunately, most companies are product-driven rather than customer-driven and maintain only transactional relationships with their customers. That is, they only connect with them when the customers buy something. Transaction-based relationships lose money all the time because *they don't leverage their connection with their customers.*

How foolish! A *customer is like a funnel* and can accept much more than just one product or service if you "pour" them properly. But to do this, you must create and develop a long-term relationship based on value, and value-added, which is all the non-product related things you do for the customer that enrich the relationship and the interdependency between you. If you have not done it yet, figure out the average *Lifetime Value* of your customers. Then do something about making it longer and richer.

**You need to establish a relationship that goes beyond each transaction. Then leverage that relationship to offer more solutions to customer needs, other than what they usually order. When you have that kind of relationship, it is easier to find out what customers want and need.**

## HOW MANY EXISTING CUSTOMERS DOES YOUR COMPANY LOSE EVERY YEAR?

It is estimated that the average company loses about 10 percent of its existing customers every year. How much does that cost? Well, just multiply that number by the average lifetime value of your customers.

How much do you make for each existing customer that you don't lose? It is estimated that each retained customer drops an additional 5 percent to your bottom line because you would have had to spend that much, and likely more, to replace him or her. Further, getting a new customer costs 10 to 15 times more than what it costs to retain one.

**Check to see what percentage of your customer base is lost every year. Then examine the reasons and fix them. In addition, make it a point to find new ways to increase customer satisfaction.**

## How Long Does It Take to Replace an Existing Customer?

Have you ever heard of **10-10-10?** It says that it takes 10 months to gain a new customer, only 10 seconds to lose that customer, and 10 years to get him back. Granted, those figures may be exaggerated, but they do highlight the importance of retaining your customers. Further if the average company loses 10 percent of its customer base each year, replacing that loss had to be factored into the following years sales plan, plus whatever percentage of additional growth the company is planning. *Sounds challenging?* Yes, it is, and yet most companies do not build that factor into their growth plans, and, worse still, they don't concentrate on reducing their annual customer loss, which would make the growth challenge a lot easier.

On the other hand, a 2 percent increase in customer retention can increase your bottom line by as much as a 10 percent reduction in costs.

**Explain 10-10-10 to your employees, and create an incentive plan that rewards them for retaining customers**

## Can Losing A Customer Be a Good Thing?

How can losing a customer be a good thing? When customers are unprofitable, that is, you lose money every time you sell to them, logic says you would be better off without them. How much does it cost to provide service to unprofitable customers? Do you have any way of tracking customer profitabiity? It is possible that up to 50 percent of your customers might be unprofitable, and a few good ones are supporting the bad ones. A *Harvard Business Review study conducted some five years ago indicated that many companies might have that number of unprofitable customers and not know it.* What is worse is that, quite often your largest customer may be your most unprofitable one, and you can't let him go because you would have to close your plant if you did.

Start tracking customer Profitability. Find ways to make them profitable and make the hard decisions to get rid of the unprofitable ones.

## How Much Does an Unhappy, Disgruntled, or Resentful Employee Cost?

What do you do when you are unhappy, disgruntled, and resentful? I'll bet it isn't thinking about ways to improve the company (other maybe than firing your boss). Most likely, you will be less motivated and even less productive. Depending on your position within the company, the impact could be considerable. For example: What is the best way to lose customers? Have disgruntled employees treat them unpleasantly, and you not only lose the customer, but also the customers lifetime value, which could be thousands of dollars. It pays to pay attention to employee morale (although I do not know for sure how you "un-gruntle" someone who is disgruntled.)

**Remember: any one of the employees who have contact with customers can make or break your business in a matter of seconds. Double check customer complaints and how they were handled, and make sure that supervisors pay special attention to how employees treat customers. And, finally, don't make your employees unhappy. On the contrary, work at making them happy and more productive.**

## The Tip of The Money-Losing Iceberg

Is all this information about ways that companies lose money without realizing it *scary*? You bet it is. But what is really scary is that *it is only the tip of the iceberg*. Like the iceberg, beyond what we have presented here, there is so much more underwater that no one realizes. And, like the iceberg, as the volatile winds of the marketplace continue to shift and the climate gets warmer, *those companies will melt away*

**Just as there are myriad ways of losing money, there are just as many or more ways to make more money by doing the right things for your customers**

*Question. When was the last time you fired a customer? If you haven't, you can be sure you have customers that cost you more than what they generate in profits for you.*

## Lowering Costs of Goods & Cycle Time

### You Can Do Better!

Here is a thought for you: Revenues come from outside the company. *Everything inside the company is a cost.* The greater the difference you can create between your revenue and your costs, the greater your profits.

It seems to be a simple, logical conclusion. If so, then why do companies continually forget it? They tend to concentrate the greater part of their time, efforts, thinking, and money internally instead of externally where the revenues come from.

Lowering Cost of Goods is not an occasional project. No matter how much sales revenues may be increasing, the effort to lower costs should never stop or even slow down because it is essential to growing Gross Profits. Further, reducing costs should be the responsibility of every employee.

## Cycle Time

Which area of operations is costing most may surprise you when you analyze them? I remember asking one of my consulting clients how long their production cycle took from order entry to dispatching. They said it took 8 days. I asked why, and was told, "That is what it has always taken."

I decided to analyze the process. Most of the orders came by telephone through Order Entry, where a woman took the information, asked a few questions, filled out the order form, and put it in the Out-Box. I then asked where does it go from here?"

"It goes to Inventory Control to determine if we have the necessary raw materials or if we need to order them" she said. I asked, "Who?" She pointed to a man on the other side of the room.

"How does it get here from there?"

"He comes by at the end of the day and picks up all the orders", was her reply.

The other side of the room was only 15 feet away, but it took the orders a whole day to get there!

I then interviewed the Inventory Control man. His process was more delayed because he had to check a variety of data in different locations. But, he somehow managed to process each days' orders by the end of the second day. Having filled out the necessary information, he deposited it in his Out-Box. "Where does it go from here?", I inquired. He pointed across the street to the laboratory. I asked, "When?"

You can guess the answer: "By the end of the day."

Every place where I checked, the orders sat for a full day. They were lucky to get the orders out in eight days. By doing something as simple as moving orders right after they were processed, they could have been shipped by the end of the fourth day.

If, by reducing the time orders just sat there waiting to be moved to the next step, they had been able to ship in four days, the time they freed up would have allowed them to double their annual sales capacity.

When I showed the information to the management, they shook their heads in disbelief. "You must be mistaken." they said.

I told them that it was the real process, and that they risked losing clients by not shortening their production cycle. They disagreed and chose to keep it as it was. Four years later, they were out of business.

In manufacturing, some of the common elements of Cost of Goods are Time, Raw Materials, Equipment, Labor, Inventory, Facilities, Energy, Disposal, and, depending on the nature of the manufacturing, there can be more steps such as Design and others.

In services, Time, and People are the main considerations. How they are allocated and concentrated can make the difference between profit and loss.

## THE PARETO PRINCIPLE

We discussed this earlier, but let's take another look because it is essential for controlling costs.

**The 80/20 Law Is Back!** A minority of inputs generate the majority of output. Apply 80/20 analysis to all your company's activities. This pattern repeats itself in everything

- 20% of clients generate 80% of sales
- 20% of products generate 80% of Gross Profit
- 20% of salespeople generate 80% of sales
- 20% of products generate 80% of inventory
- 20% of activities generate 80% of costs
- 20% of raw materials generate 80% of costs

## SIMPLICITY EQUALS EFFECTIVENESS

Complexity obfuscates. That is why achieving simplicity in everything is so important. A study of 39 German mid-size companies indicated that the main thing separating the successful from the less-so was the simplicity of their operations. The successful companies sell a smaller variety of products to fewer customers and have fewer suppliers. It sounds simple, and it is; *try to simplify everything all the time.*

### Reduce Costs and Expenses

80% of your company's most important activities receive only 20% of resources, *which means that the other 80% of the resources are applied to less important activities.* Identify that least productive

80%, and concentrate on either making it more effective or getting rid of it

### Definition of "Important"

Everything that enhances the Profit of sales, products, and revenue, and creates value for customers, is important. So, what do we do with the rest?

### What we do with the rest?

These are the actions we should consider when trying to reduce expenses:

| | | |
|---|---|---|
| Eliminate | Reduce | Substitute |
| Accelerate | Delegate | Outsource |
| Synchronize | Shorten | Redesign |
| Simplify | Rent | Sell |
| Transfer | Charge | Borrow |
| Share | Distribute | Destroy |

## OTHER NORMS

- What you don't measure, you don't get. It pays to track expenditures.
- What you do not document, you don't remember.
- What is every ones' responsibility is no ones' responsibility. Make it clear who is responsible for reducing each type of cost or expense.
- What you don't negotiate, costs more. Challenge prices.

## Lowering Costs?

Lowering costs can be expensive if you try to reduce everything at the same time. Besides, when considering cost reduction analysis, it pays to look for those areas that offer the best ROI for the time, effort, and money invested in trying to lower their costs.

The logical place to seek cost reductions is in those elements that cost the most and take the most time. The simplest method for reducing costs is through conducting 80/20 analyses. Then, you need to determine which costs are strategic (contribute to the bottom line) and which are non-strategic (reduce the bottom line).

## Supplies

If you are in manufacturing, for example, the larger percentage costs are likely to be in supplies. First you need to identify that 80 percent that costs the most, and then determine how you can reduce it

What do you buy the most of? Whatever it is, that is where to look for cost reductions. Here are some questions you can ask:

## Cost Reduction Questions

- Are you using too much?
- Are you paying too much?
- Are you buying from only one source?
- Do you really need it?
- Can you replace it with something less expensive?
- Can you eliminate it?
- Can you import it cheaper?
- Can you combine or bundle it with other purchases at a lower price?
- Can you re-negotiate prices and terms? Are there better alternatives?

- Is shipping too expensive?
- Would it be less expensive if you bought it in larger quantities?
- Would it be less expensive if you bought it in larger quantities over a longer period?
- Can you get more help and services from the supplier?
- Can you pool resources with other buyers of the same products to get greater volume discounts?
- Can you get the supplier to stock it nearby?
- Can you outsource part of the operation to a supplier?
- Can you produce your own version?
- Should you buy out the supplier?
- Can you redesign or reformulate the product to be less expensive?
- Can you re-sell what you don't use?
- Can you negotiate better prices and terms?
- Are you using a better quality than needed?
- Is there a more efficient process that would use less of the product?
- Can you dilute it more?
- Can you produce it yourself?
- Is there a different version that might actually save money because you would use much less?
- Can you get on-time delivery that would save money because you would not need as much inventory?

## SUPPLIERS

The second part of lowering the cost of supplies is selecting and negotiating with suppliers. Purchased goods are the target. Let's look at the impact of a 5 percent reduction of the prices of your purchased goods.

| | |
|---|---|
| Sales | $1,000,000 |
| COG | 700,000 |
| GP | 300,000 |

Assume purchased goods represent 80 percent of Sustainable Cost of Goods, or $700,000 X.80 = $560,000. If we can reduce the prices we are paying for purchased goods by 5 percent, here is what we would get: $560,000 X .05 = $28,000. Our Gross Profit would now be $328,000, a 9 percent increase. How much additional sales would it take to generate that Goss Profit increase?

If our General Sales and Administrative expenses (GSA) represented 25 percent of Revenues, or $250,000, our bottom would be $50,000. By adding $28,000 to our Gross Profit, we now add that same amount to our bottom line, and we have grown it from 5 percent of Revenues to 7.8 percent.

If you think that a 2.8 percent increase of the bottom line is not much, consider this: First, that getting an extra $28,000 to the bottom line would require selling an additional $300,000 of sales, a sales increase of 30 percent which is not easy in any market. Second, rising from $50,000 to $78,000 profits represent a 56 percent increase, no small matter.

| | | | |
|---|---|---|---|
| Sales | $1,000,000 | Sales | $1,000,000 |
| COG | 700,000 | COG | 672,000 |
| GP | 300,000 | GP | 328,000 |
| GSA | 250,000 | GSA | 250,000 |
| Profit | 50,000 | Profit | 78,000 |

Now, how hard is it to get a 5 percent reduction in prices from suppliers? You will never know until you try, but it may be a lot easier than you think.

- Start by renegotiating existing prices.
- Look at buying in higher quantities if you have the storage space.
- Set target price goals for each vendor; some of them can be higher than 5 percent.
- Take aim at largest suppliers first.
- Before actually entering into negotiations, ask for bids from their competitors.
- Keep asking. Keep negotiating.

Even if you don't reach your overall targeted price reduction goal, whatever you get will increase your bottom line without having to raise sales. Keep in mind, however, that average annual inflation runs about 4 percent, which means two key things:

1. Your costs and expenses will tend to increase proportionally, therefore, you need to reduce both continually.
2. You need to raise your prices every year by at least that much just to stay even Manufacturing

Places to look for cost reductions. Get your team together and ask them these questions. Have someone write answers down, and then ask, "What are you going to do about it?

## COST REDUCTION QUESTIONS

Where are you:

- Spending the most?
- Investing the most?
- Using the most energy?
- Devoting the most labor?
- Consuming the most time?
- Causing the most problems?

- Generating the most rejects?
- Taking up the most space?
- Producing the least results?
- Finding it harder and more expensive to operate?

For example, in manufacturing what processes take the most time?

Sometimes, lengthy processes may actually represent only a minor part of the manufacturing; they might contribute little, yet cost a lot. For example, in manufacturing where paint is applied to the product:

- How long does the drying in an oven take?
- What if the product requires several coats of different paints?
- How much is the total oven time?
- Does the product have to go around several times to pass through the same oven, or does it require several ovens which consume large amounts of energy and take up a large amount of space?

Some equipment takes longer to set up or maintain.

- If one line is used for manufacturing several products, does the equipment have to be re-set each time, and how long does that take?
- What is the cost of the downtime?

Other types of equipment may be very expensive, but aren't used that much.

- Is 80 percent of the investment in equipment that is used for only 20 percent of the time?
- Can this be outsourced?

Some equipment may be too hard to control and manage, thereby requiring frequent adjustments. What does the down time cost?

There is a tendency in many manufacturing operations to continue using obsolete equipment even if it is less productive than newer technologies. What is the loss of productivity of such a decision?

Equipment layouts may not be as efficient as they need to be. Ideally, production should flow efficiently from beginning to end. The inefficient layout may be costing more money because of time losses.

Product specifications are often outdated, and cost more than they should. Some specifications have remained unchanged for more than 20 years. Are they still valid? Are they too low? Are they too high? Technology has changed enormously during that period, and it may be possible to set higher specifications that result in better products and easier production.

Are workers as efficient as they could be? Is their time being used properly? What are they doing, or could be doing, when the line is down?

Are workers demoralized? Unhappy people do not produce happy results. Motivation should be a daily matter, not just something occasional. It pays to pay attention to your worker needs. Motivated people are far more likely to be productive workers, and higher productivity ends up lowering your costs and increasing your profits.

## DELIVERIES

Getting the product to the customer can sometimes be a costly process. Questions you might ask:

- Can you outsource delivery and get even better results?
- Can you get customers to buy larger amounts so that you have fewer deliveries?

- Do you have the most efficient delivery vehicles?
- Do you have a standard rate for shipping, or one that varies according to the distance?
- Do you own your vehicles outright, or do you lease them?
- Are your vehicle maintenance costs too high?
- Can you program and plan your deliveries more efficiently to reduce number of trips and mileage?
- Is cargo space efficiently allocated for maximum loading?
- Is the shipping dock properly designed for fastest loading and unloading?
- Are drivers properly trained to choose best delivery routes?
- Do vehicle insurance plans provide adequate coverage at a good price?
- Should you consider increasing order size to reduce the number of unprofitable deliveries?
- Should you charge proportionately more for smaller order deliveries than larger ones?
- Are you charging enough for special deliveries?
- Do you allow or encourage customer pick-up of their orders?
- Do you plan deliveries so drivers can pick up supplies on their return trips?
- Is your staff knowledgeable enough to handle international orders and deliveries?

## ENERGY

Energy costs are becoming a growing cost factor and need careful attention. Currently, there are no inexpensive sources of energy, and one thing is for sure – there will not be any in the short run. Granted, wind is free and so is sunshine, but the cost of making them available is considerable. Coal is relatively cheaper than oil, but controlling its pollution impact is expensive. It pays to monitor energy costs closely, accumulate solid data, and look for better, less expensive alternatives.

- Do you analyze your energy costs on a regular basis?
- Have you designed an energy master plan for your business?
- Do you know where your energy is being used and how much?
- Do you have energy-saving policies and procedures?
- Are all the lights on in your building all night?
- Are you moving towards alternative energy sources?
- Do you have shades or blinds to keep out the hot summer sun?
- Have you checked windows and doors for leaks that admit cold air in the winter, or let cold air out during the summer?
- Are you recovering any of the energy being spent?
- How many pieces of equipment are left on all night?
- Do the temperature controls work properly? Or, does your place get so cold in the summer that employees have to open doors to let warm air in?
- Are there parts of the building where the circulation is inadequate and are too cold in the winter and too hot in the summer?
- Is the air in your plant clean?
- Is the lighting in your building adequate or does it cause eye strain?
- Are there enough electrical outlets for the growing amount of electronic equipment required in today's business?
- Are you looking for ways to automate more tasks?
- Is anyone in your organization in charge of monitoring energy consumption?
- Have you considered switching your vehicles from fossil fuels to hybrids and other alternatives?
- Have you increased insulation as a way to lower both heating and air conditioning costs?
- Are you renegotiating energy contracts to obtain lower costs?
- Why not buy larger-than-you-need volumes of gasoline at

SUSTAINABLE PROFIT GROWTH

lower prices, and share the excess with the employees offering them lower than gas station prices?

- Are you recycling water, and using it for non-drinking purposes?
- Are you collecting rain water?
- Are you selling some waste products such as metals and paper to businesses that use them for their own production?

## Summary

When it comes to reducing costs, the reality is that everything may be obtained at a lower price, be used more efficiently, and disposed of more productively. But this can only happen if everything and everyone is consciously looking for opportunities to increase Profit by lowering cost of goods.

*Question. Would you agree that all the questions in the above lists should be asked sooner or later and probably several times a year? If you do agree, then print the lists out and share them with your team.*

**Note.** You can do better - is a phrase used in negotiating prices. If you are buying and the vendor offers a price that you think is too high, you say, "You can do better." The advantage of this phrase is that it usually leads to the vendor lowering the price. Then you can use your phrase again and see if he will go even lower. If you are the vendor, and a customer offers too little, say the phrase and it might get him or her to come up higher.

# CHAPTER EIGHT
# Reducing Expenses Are You Getting Your Money's Worth?

Expenses tend to increase automatically every year in many subtle but costly ways. If areas such as services, office supplies, technology, communications, subscriptions, energy, office equipment, travel, entertainment and, most important of all, people effectiveness, are not measured and analyzed on a regular basis, they will substantially undermine Profit.

Management, Sales, and Administrative expenses tend to rise constantly. It's almost like they have a sneaky power of their own to get out of control. The questions you need to ask yourself are very much like the ones in the previous chapter regarding lowering Cost of Goods with a few differences.

- What do you buy the most of? Whatever it is, that is where to look for expense reductions.
- Are you using too much?
- Are you paying too much?
- Are you buying from only one source?
- Do you really need it?
- Can you replace it with something less expensive?
- Can you eliminate it?
- Can you import it cheaper?
- Can you combine or bundle it with other purchases at a lower price?
- Can you re-negotiate prices and terms? Are there better alternatives?
- Is shipping too expensive?
- Would it be less expensive if you bought it in larger quantities?

- Would it be less expensive if you bought it in larger quantities over a longer period?
- Can you get more help and services from the supplier?
- Can you pool resources with other buyers of the same products to get greater volume discounts?
- Can you get the supplier to stock it nearby?
- Can you outsource part of the operation to a supplier?
- Can you produce your own version?
- Should you buy out the supplier?
- Can you redesign or reformulate the product to be less expensive?
- Can you re-sell what you don't use?
- Can you negotiate better prices and terms?
- Are you using a better quality than needed?
- Is there a more efficient process that would use less of the product?
- Can you dilute it more?
- Can you produce it yourself?
- Is there a different version that might actually save money because you would use much less?
- Can you get just-on-time delivery that would save money because you would not need as much inventory?

Now add to this list the following items:

- What are you spending on subscriptions?
- How many telephones do you really need?
- Can they be just basic rather than sophisticated?
- What are you paying in telephone bills monthly?
- Can you get better rates by shopping around a little more?
- How many of your employees really need cellular phones?
- What kind?
- Do you need all the space you are currently using?
- Do you really need a reception area and function?

- Are you better off renting rather than investing?
- Are you paying more for a centrally located facility?
- Could you be located in a less expensive area?
- How much of the travel you are paying for is unnecessary?
- Are you paying too much for office equipment maintenance contracts?
- Do local salespeople really need desks?
- Could salespeople work remotely?
- How much of your office processing (such as order entry) is still done manually rather than being automated, or at least digital?
- How much of your office processing is really necessary?
- What percentage of paper reports could be reduced?
- How many people have company cars? Should they?
- How many people have expense accounts? Should they?
- How often do you review office supply contracts?
- Are there any that you can eliminate?
- How many of your people are authorized to make purchases?
- How often do you review their records?
- How many of your people are authorized for signing checks?
- How often do you review their records?
- How many computers are there in your offices?
- Do you need that many?
- How many need to be sophisticated, cutting edge technology?
- What is the percentage of usage of office computers?
- How much software do you really need?
- Which people need which kinds?
- Does anybody monitor the ways computers are being used?
- How much is office cleaning and maintenance costing?
- Are there better options?
- How many copiers do you need?
- How many printers?
- What kinds?
- Do you review expense accounts?

- Do you review sales reports?
- How many managers do you have?
- Do you need them all?
- How many administrative assistants do you have?
- Do you need them all?
- How many temporaries?

Note. Copy these lists and share them throughout the organization.

## THE PEOPLE PART OF EXPENSES

- Companies are mostly people, and only as good as the quality of their people. People are expensive, but good people are invaluable. Therefore, hiring good people may seem expensive, but a well-run company that measures performance based on their contribution to Profit will continually improve its ROI.
- It is your job to create a profit-oriented culture within your organization. By "culture" I mean the values and practices that the company encourages and rewards.
- It should be clear to all employees, from yourself to the security guard (if you have one) that the purpose of the company is to produce an increasingly healthy profit by supplying the best value for the dollar to every profitable customer. By "profitable customers," I mean those who bring in more money than they cost.
- Employees must understand that they are expected to produce more than they cost. They must also realize that reducing costs and expenses and generating profits are part of their job too, and that they will be measured and rewarded in proportion to their contribution to that objective.
- It is also your job to make sure that high standards are set for every employee. At the same time, however, you must also create and communicate a clear vision of the company's

future path, and motivate all employees by constantly pointing out (and delivering) the rewards they will receive as they help make that future real.

- If you are going to demand a lot out of your people (and you should), they deserve a generous reward. You can't motivate people to generate higher profits while paying them little. That does not mean that rewards should become widespread and automatically expected. For example, if bonuses are given regularly regardless of performance, not only will they become expected, they will also be discounted.
- Compensation should remain tied to performance. The jobs that contribute the most and most directly to Profit should be better paid than those that contribute less directly. Of course, there will be noticeable differences between salaries as related to performance and profit impact. No employee, however, should ever be considered indispensable. As mentioned earlier, French General Charles De Gaulle made a good point, *"The cemeteries are filled with indispensable men."*

*Question. Based on a hypothetical situation that we outlined earlier, if the number of our employees increased 15 percent over the last two years, what measures are you going to take to reduce that increase? Have you identified the productive from the unproductive employees? What problems do you anticipate when you start cutting personnel?*

*Question. Your union's contract is coming for negotiation in six months, have you started preparing for this? What are some of the things you need to do between now and then?*

**Note.** Negotiating is not a topic of this book, but here are some things you may want to think about:

- Who will conduct the negotiations with the union?
- Have they had training in negotiation?
- What things have changed since the last negotiation?

- How might they affect these negotiations?
- What new issues might the union bring up?
- What have other unions in your industry and region been demanding?
- What issues do you want to bring up?
- Where do you have room to accept changes?
- What can you demand in exchange?
- What issues are critical?
- What issues are not negotiable?
- What will the cost of a new contract represent?
- At what point would a strike be preferable to an unacceptable contract?

## SUMMARY

There are lots of places where you can reduce expenses, provided you set measurable expense reduction goals, and you and your team constantly look for them.

You cannot see what you don't look for and you cannot look for what you don't believe in.

Believe that there are always lots of places where you can reduce expenses with a positive impact on the bottom line, and you will always be able to look for and find them.

## LEVERAGING RESOURCES

*"If you count all your assets, you always show a profit."*
*Robert Quillen*

## Sitting on Your Assets?

Ever been to an Estate Sale? That is where, presumably, what is being sold is from the estate of someone who has passed away. The amount of property is almost overwhelming, so much so that you cannot help but wonder how much of it was actually used on a regular basis. The business equivalent of an Estate Sale is a Bankruptcy Sale. Again, you wonder why the deceased company needed so much. Perhaps, if the deceased company had not held on to so much that was seldom if ever used, it would not have entered bankruptcy.

The message is that you do not have a genuine need for everything you own. In addition, you are probably not getting as much value out of everything as you should. In other words, wasted money is sitting around unproductive while capital is probably scarce. Therefore, to increase your profits, give serious consideration to getting the most out of everything, that is, leverage your resources to the max!

## Resource Leveraging Principles

**All the company's assets must generate profits.** Generating profits is what assets are supposed to be used for. This is easy to forget, and that is one of the key reasons why it should be remembered. Assets are a means not a purpose. When assets generate more costs than profits, they should be analyzed as to how they contribute to that goal. All assets must perform more than one function and do it 24 hours. This is hard to do, but if you make it a habit to consider this option consistently, you will come up with some very creative moves that could save, or generate, millions of dollars.

# WORST INVESTMENT? MANAGEMENT EGO!

Corporate jets, palatial offices, fancy lodging, company vehicles, luxurious furniture, gourmet meals, and all other accessories of corporate ego, tend to substantially increase cost with little or no return on investments. They tend to distract and corrupt cultures of Profit.

## YOU DON'T HAVE TO OWN EVERYTHING YOU USE OR NEED

Think about it. Owning is not necessarily vital to the company interest. Many times renting, leasing, outsourcing, and other less expensive options than owning, can be a wise move that will create more cash availability.

## RESOURCES DO NOT BELONG TO ANY ONE DEPARTMENT BUT TO THE WHOLE COMPANY

Departments and divisions tend to become possessive about their assets. Many times, such attitude ends up causing more investment in unnecessary assets.

**Marketing strategies must not be based on protecting assets. The purpose of a business is not to run a plant, but to create and delight customers while making a worthwhile profit. When CEO's begin to make decisions about marketing based exclusively on keeping plants running, they inevitably lose their competitive edge.**

This chapter is about getting the most out of everything you've got -- and more! Every business has capital invested in:

- Space
- Equipment
- Paid service
- Research
- Advertising

- Promotion
- Software
- Furniture
- Technology
- Boards of directors
- Memberships
- Inventories

**Question: As you examine each of these areas, ask yourself, "Does this investment contribute to increasing revenues, or to the bottom line?" If it doesn't, then there are six options you must consider:**

- Make it contribute.
- Leverage it.
- Sell it.
- Rent it out.
- License it.
- Get rid of it.

As we go through each of the categories of invested capital, we will review the six questions listed above. Some of the suggestions in the following pages may not apply to your specific industry, but may trigger some creative thinking.

## SPACE

Space is something you own or rent 24/7 365 days a year. How much of that time do you use that space? Given a normal 40hour workweek times 52 weeks a year that equals 2,080 hours out of a Sustainable you pay for of 8,760 hours a year, or only 23.7 percent. Space is usually a low return investment.

**Make it contribute.** How? If it is a plant, you can have two or three shifts, provided you can generate enough business to fill the shifts. If it is an office, that is less likely, but certain operations may lend themselves to shifts. But, do you actually need all the space you have? Are you performing functions that could be outsourced?

A law firm in London sends all its typing and transcribing needs to India overnight. When the London lawyers arrive in the morning, all the typing and transcribing is done and awaiting. Does this reduce the need for space in the London office? Quite possibly.

- **Leverage it.** On a temporary basis, it might be possible to let clients use unused space when they need it in that area. This would come under the heading of Value-Added benefits for clients. Recently, when I was conducting a seminar for a client at their law firms' office in between presentations, I needed to handle an hour and a half long conference call. The law firm graciously loaned me a conference room to take that call. The space was not being used, so they allowed me to use it as a way of building client relationship.
- **Sell it.** If you own unused space, why not sell it? If you can't sell it, maybe you can barter it for some sort of service.
- **Rent it out.** Renting out unused space should be easy, unless there is a problem with the configuration of that space. Of course, if that is the case, you might consider remodeling it either to make it useful to your business or for renting out. Another possibility could be to rent it out for meeting or training purposes. There is hardly ever an oversupply of conference rooms. You could also rent out the space as individual temporary offices or for young companies and entrepreneurs.
- **Get rid of it.** Sometimes you can do so by selling it as mentioned above. If all other options fail, you can always move to a smaller, less expensive location.

**Note.** You can reduce the amount of office space needed by increasing the number of employees who could work from home.

## Equipment

Equipment is usually purchased to produce something or solve a need or a problem. What if the something could be produced elsewhere by somebody else? What if the need is not essential? What if the problem could be eliminated or outsourced?

- **Make it contribute.** The functionality of a piece of equipment lies in its throughput. How much do you use it? If it is part of production, the challenge becomes scheduling enough production through that particular piece of equipment. Management needs to determine if the products manufactured on that piece of equipment are essential to revenue and profit generation. If they are not a key part of a product line, then perhaps those products should be discontinued This is another reason why management must regularly review product line performance in the market.

- If the piece of equipment is for office use, the degree of its usage should determine its degree of necessity. Sometimes, something as simple as a mere change of location within the office can result in more throughput. A copier, for example, is both a necessity and a convenience. Most copiers tend to last a long time, while the amount of work tends to increase with the passing of time. Rather than have two copiers to deal with the increasing work, why not buy a copier with much greater capacity and sell the old one? You don't think you could find a buyer for it? You would be surprised how many start-up businesses are out there that would be interested in buying your old copier.

- **Leverage it.** As mentioned above, a change of location can often increase usage. All too often, equipment usage is limited to a narrow range of needs, while it may be able to serve a wider variety. Most people never study the instructions or user manuals where the possibilities of additional uses are often listed. For example, how many of the buttons on the dashboard of your car, do you use to their fullest extent? In many cases, a few modifications of current equipment can open a whole world of additional applications.

- **Sell it.** Old equipment is usually relatively easy to sell either for the same type of use, or as scrap for its metallic content. The important thing is to make sure that somebody in the company has responsibility for this function.

- **Rent it out.** Depending on the nature of the equipment, sometimes it is possible to rent it out without having to change its location. Your copier could provide a copying service to other offices in the same building. Photographic equipment can provide a plethora of services that generate revenues. As rentals, trucks can provide for many "end" uses. Again, somebody within the organization needs to take charge of these possibilities.

- **License it.** Executive jets are often leased out to others. The same could be done with trucks that are reaching an age where they no longer serve your company's requirements, but could still be very useful to smaller companies.

- **Get rid of it.** It is rather common to retain equipment way beyond its point of obsolescence simply because it still works. As a matter of fact, this is very common in Third World countries. But obsolete equipment may be costing you more than it is producing. Because of the "it still works" bias, it may be wise to bring in an outside technical expert periodically to review the relative obsolescence of your equipment.

## PAID SERVICES

Every business finds itself paying for a wide range of services for an even wider range of purposes that supposedly are needed to maintain functionality and effectiveness. Such things as cleaning, servicing equipment, payroll management, training, consulting, bookkeeping, auditing, web site design and maintenance, computer backup, and so on. As a rule, the need for and the quality of these services should be reviewed at least annually to determine if the service is still needed, could be improved, or should be re-negotiated.

- **Make it contribute.** After a period of time, many service providers tend to take their clients for granted. They get into performance rituals that become ruts, and nobody pays attention to their performance, or lack of it, because the service providers have been there —forever. Companies should get periodic feedback from employees regarding service performance quality. This should be a responsibility of supervisors, administrators, and managers, essentially your team, and the information should be shared with all employees.
- **Leverage it.** The people who provide you with services also do so with other companies where they see and learn many things that could be helpful to you. Why not consult with them about ways to improve things, and also to connect you with companies of interest as potential clients?
- **Sell it.** You can't sell the services that others provide for you – or can you? If the service could benefit some of your clients, why not enter into an alliance with the provider to offer that service? If nothing else, by connecting your service providers with potential clients you might get a special price from them.
- **Rent it out.** The same possibilities mentioned in the preceding paragraph could apply here.
- **License it.** Depending on the nature of the service provided, as part of the alliance you might create a franchising operation with mutual benefit for you and your supplier.
- **Get rid of it.** Some services may be retained their usefulness simply because they are there. Ask your team to help you

review your current list of services and service providers to determine if they are still needed or should be replaced.

## RESEARCH

Any type of research is usually costly and should provide more than one benefit. Often times, the information developed through research will be valuable to others and therefore saleable.

- **Make it contribute.** All too often research ends up being an endless source of expense with little return. Part of the problem lies in several key elements of research:
  - o Inadequate definition of the goal and expectations. As Yogi Berra put it, "If you don't know where you are going, you won't know when you get there."
  - o A sense of urgency: without deadlines, things don't progress.
  - o Developing a prototype: you need something tangible that people can experience.
  - o Getting quality feedback: never assume you know all the answers.
  - o Lack of depth: surveys – a form of research – are frequently too superficial. Customers are asked for opinions, but no probing is done to determine the thinking and reasoning behind them.
  - o Not paying more attention to side effect discoveries. Research often discovers a lot of unexpected surprises that may not contribute to the specific goal of the research but have the potential for new inventions and innovations.
- **Leverage it.** What other things can you derive from the research process? Research lends itself to training of future researchers, or just to educate related personnel to the basics of the specific science or art. Some invention processes are

made up of several steps each of which could become a separate product, process, or patentable innovation.

- **Sell it.** The information obtained from research and surveys may be saleable to other companies and industries. Again, saleable White Papers can also be developed based on research and surveys. We tend to forget that knowledge is saleable.
- **Rent it out.** Once you have developed a research process and have an experienced team, you can take on projects for others. For example, you could ally with other companies in the industry to do research for them that also benefits your business.
- **License it.** I recently visited a company that prides itself on its ability to develop creative solutions for its clients. On the wall of their conference room were copies of several of their inventions that they had patented. I asked the CEO if they had ever licensed this knowledge to other companies in the United States and abroad. He looked surprised. Apparently, in all the years the company had been operating, no one had thought of that potential revenue stream.
- **Get rid of it.** By all means. If it isn't working, farm it out! However, if you outsource research, remember to focus on the key elements indicated above under *Make it work*.

### ADVERTISING

Famous retailer and entrepreneur John Wanamaker said, "I know that half of my advertising is wasted. Unfortunately, I don't know which half." To get a feeling for how wasteful advertising can be, just try to remember the commercials you saw on TV last night. When you see some commercials, don't you ever wonder what on earth they were thinking of when they put that ad together?

- **Make it contribute.** Too many ads and commercials are product driven; they focus on the features of the products or services without even mentioning the related benefits which, after all, the real reason for making purchases. Appeal to emotions, more than logic, because buying is emotional.

- **Set goals for advertising.** I once challenged an ad suggested by the creative director of a famous agency because I did not see how it would increase sales. Irritated, he said, "Do not be so prosaic." My response was, "If you are not prosaic, I guess you don't think of getting paid for your work." My point was that even advertising must have a bottom line.

- **Leverage it.** Even though advertising should be narrowly targeted, you can make sure it does several things such as sell the product or service, strengthen your brand, get the customer involved (coupons, rebates, raffles, awards, prizes, etc.), differentiate your brand, product, and company, provide feedback and get recognition. You can also get your distributors to contribute by involving them. Some companies very cleverly alert customers to new products coming down the road while advertising existing ones.

- **Sell it.** You may be wondering how you could possibly sell advertising without becoming an advertising agency or a form of media. Well, have you ever thought of forming an advertising co-operative? A co-op is basically an alliance which can include other companies in the same business but not necessarily direct competitors, plus suppliers, and sometimes even customers.

- **Merchandising.** Occasionally, a series of ads or commercials makes something fashionable and, in the process, allows the advertising company to get into merchandising as do movies, TV shows, and some products. McDonald's has used cartoon and other movie characters to sell its products.

- **Rent it out.** This is exactly what truck rentals do when they rent out their vehicles with their brand name blazoned on the side, back, and even front of it.

- **License it.** That Is what franchising is all about. You are licensing the use of a business system, and your brand name which every franchisee should include in everything it does.

- **Get rid of it.** It may be that advertising is not the best way of making your business known. Other resources may be more effective like having a good web site. It is one of the most powerful forms of advertising and product promotion today. Plus, do not ignore packaging as another powerful form of advertising. When you stop to think about it, advertising is just one of several ways of getting your message across to potential customers.

## PROMOTION

I include promotion as a separate consideration because it combines the Big 3 Ps: Promotion, Publicity, and Public Relations. There are many ways of building brands, recognition, and even sales with these systems. In all cases, one of the keys to success is a fourth P: Positioning, which is creating a carefully crafted perception in the minds of customers and the public in general. It is easy to spend enormous amounts of money on these efforts without achieving anything, and a lot of companies do just that. That is why clear definition of purpose, goals, and perception are essential to getting the right results. And, above all, it is vital to have, and maintain, focus throughout.

- **Make it contribute.** If it does not achieve the goal, why do it at all? Every one of the 3 Ps requires well defined goals and targets. If you are looking for recognition of your brand, how many ways are there of getting it out there at no cost? Press releases, newsletters, blogs, participation in worthy causes, interviews by the media (assuming you have something worth being interviewed for), public speaking, conferences, trade shows, writing articles, networking, samples (these do cost), and just showing up at events.

- **Leverage it.** Properly applied clever creativity can leverage all of the 3 Ps by generating buzz. Look at how much publicity Apple gets when it introduces a new product and people camp out in front of their stores days in advance just to spend their money acquiring the latest innovation.
- **Sell it.** If you do it right, there are numerous ways of placing products and services for sale in many venues. When General Motors (not the best example of selling, but occasionally successful) launched its Saturn brand, buyers actually formed owner clubs which, if managed right, could have been built into a great way to sell more vehicles. (Too bad GM shot itself in the foot by downplaying Saturn). But Harley Davidson saved their company by forming clubs.
- **Rent it out.** On occasions, some companies have leased out sections of their stores to non-competing products and services. For example, supermarkets have leased space to banks. This is a case where both parties benefit from one-another's images and reputations.
- **License it.** Once again, franchising might serve as a way to generate profits through the combination of licensing your brand and your business model.
- **Get rid of it.** Many times, promotions, forms of publicity and public relations become traditions and rituals, "We have always done it." Unless they are evaluated regularly for their impact and effectiveness, they can become expensive non-producers, in which case it may be time to either reinvigorate them or get rid of them.

## SOFTWARE

We all work with software and often end up buying both new software and upgrades. Do we really need all the software we get? Further, do we really need to update it, which often happens automatically if we do not pay attention to our credit card statements where the automatic charges add up. Then, there is the question of what percentage of the software applications do we really use? Most likely, we use only a fraction of it.

- **Make it contribute.** At some point, it may be worth your while to find out how much software you have, what kinds, what they are supposed to do, do they do it, and how much do you use them. You and your staff might be able to increase your productivity by getting a little training on how to make better use of your software. Find out who on your staff is really sharp in this area and have him/her train the rest.
- **Leverage it.** How many people use the same software? Some software may be more specialized with only a few persons using it within the organization, but do more people have it and don't use it? Can more than one person use the same computer? Does everybody need a computer full time? By the way, do you need to buy only new computers for everyone, or can some people use refurbished ones?
- **Sell it.** It is not likely that you can sell the software you are using, unless it was designed specifically for your company. But perhaps, you could sell the service that the software makes possible.
- **Rent it out.** Essentially, this is what business centers at hotels do. For a price, they allow people to use their computers and the software on them.
- **Get rid of it.** It probably is not wise to use too many obsolete computers simply because they will lessen productivity and may not be supported by their vendors.

## FURNITURE

The natural inclination is to furnish your business with good looking, functional, and maybe even ergonomic furniture. As you may have noticed, it is expensive. So, it becomes important to determine exactly how much furniture do you really need, how many filing cabinets, shelves, lamps, etc. When you get right down to it, desks are nothing but tables with drawers, and tables are nothing but boards with legs. Cubicles are nothing but panels, and the desks within them, are often only small filing cabinets with boards on top of them. The point is, you do not need to accept existing furniture industry standards when you keep the above basics in mind. Of course, you would like to apply these with good taste, and that is what paint and special surfaces are for.

- **Make it contribute.** Everyone needs a desk? Example, sales-people are supposed to devote the majority of time to being in front of prospects and customers. Does the reception area require lounge chairs? In the age of computers, do we need so many filing cabinets? What is in those filing cabinets, and how often do you purge them of old files? Buy new? Offices and businesses are constantly going out of business; guess what they do with their furniture and equipment? They sell it, and do so at lower prices. By just giving some additional thought and planning to layouts and furnishings you can save a lot of money.

- **Leverage it.** Most furniture just sits there 24 hours a day, and is only used for 8 or even less. How might you leverage it for greater productivity? You would be amazed at just how ingenious people can be when under pressure for financial or other reasons. Not that I recommend it, but are you aware that some congressmen in Washington D.C. actually sleep in their offices rather than rent expensive D.C space? Encourage the members of your team to give some thought to more ways to leverage everything.

- **Sell it.** That doesn't mean you have to sell everything you have in your offices and plants, but if you are buying used equipment and furniture from a going-out-of-business sale, you could probably get a substantial reduction in price if you bought everything they want to get rid of. You might say,␣But I don't need everything they are selling. Of course, you don't, but you can re-sell what you don't need, and probably do so at a better price than you paid for it. And, if you are going to dispose of some old furniture, why not sell it rather than trash it. If that is too much trouble, then why not donate it to a worthy cause, and get a tax deduction at the same time?

- **Rent it out.** If you have furniture that is in the way, but may need it at a later time, instead of paying for storage, why not rent it out? As I mentioned before, if you have conference rooms, they may be a potential source of revenue.

- **Get rid of it.** Basically, sell it rather than trash it but, if you do not need it, at least find a way to make it contribute to your bottom line in the process.

## TECHNOLOGY

Most companies often do not realize the value of the solutions they create during every-day business. Not too long ago, while reviewing the operations of a company that manufactures enclosures (like bottle caps, and other dispensing devices on different types of packaging), I was amazed by the cleverness and creativity of some of the solutions they had developed for their customers. For some reason, it had never occurred to them that they could also sell these solutions to many diverse companies around the world.

- **Make it contribute.** Do not underestimate the value of your solutions. Many businesses around the world have experienced, and are probably still dealing with, similar problems. Take a good hard look at the problems you have solved internally and for your customers. You may be sitting on a potential revenue stream and not realize it. One of my clients, a chemical coatings company, had developed a special application coating for the inside of food and beverage cans.

The specifications were extremely tight given the potential health problems that could occur if the coating failed, but the technology of the coating itself was quite simple and had been around for a good number of years. You would have thought it would be obsolete by now, but that company had a wonderful revenue stream from licensing this rather old technology to businesses in 57 countries.

- **Leverage it.** From time to time, it is a good idea to see how customers are using your products and services. The Reason? Customers often come up with new and clever ways of using your products and services.
- **Sell it.** Your technology is most likely saleable. The question is, to whom: customers, suppliers, competitors, foreign entities, governments, institutions, entrepreneurs and, depending on the nature of the technology, to almost everyone. Also saleable are the skills, procedures, and processes that go with the technology. Training can be profitable and also bring in customers.
- **Rent it out or License it.** How would you like to be receiving money from licensees in 57 countries like my client did? Incredibly, that did not require a lot of time, money, and effort on the part of my client. It was "easy" money. Get your team to focus on this potential revenue stream and come with yet another solution, but one that favors your bottom line.
- **Get rid of it.** Don't. You never know who needs that technology.

Sometimes, the technology and the related skills can be combined to offer a manufacturing or assembly solution. Some years ago, a company in Quebec, Canada, that supplied door handles to the automotive industry was called in by a large client in Detroit. Their problem was that workers fitting the door handles into the doors on the assembly line, complained that they were too hard to install. The supplier looked at the door assembly process, turned to the auto executive and suggested that his company could save them a lot of time and effort by assembling the entire door for them. For the auto company the door assembly was a continuous source of problems, so they gave the business to the supplier. Never underestimate the power of your problem-solving skills.

## BOARDS OF DIRECTORS

Boards of directors are usually viewed as highly talented and experienced advisors who meet periodically to guide the company and its decisions. Most directors are indeed talented and experienced, yet companies tend to bog them down with mundane operational issues that really should be solved at a different level. Instead, Board Directors should be tapped for their insight, leadership, strategic thinking, and foresight. Over the years, experienced people develop a valuable intuition that tells them what is right, when and where. Companies should learn how to capitalize on this resource.

- **Make it contribute.** Ever since the introduction of Sarbanes/Oxley, boards have tended to focus more on compliance than on strategy. Granted, compliance is important but, unfortunately, it is more focused on the past (which is unchangeable) rather than on the future, which is malleable. The CEO should devote time to using Board Directors as sounding boards for diagnosing problems and developing innovative solutions.
- **Leverage it.** Over the years, most Board Directors have developed powerful relationships and networks that could help the company in many ways, if it strategically sought to leverage those connections.
- **Sell it.** Companies miss a wonderful public relations opportunity when they do not sell the qualities of the board to investors, employees, and customers. The company works

hard to bring together a truly powerful group of business executives and entrepreneurs as Directors, and then ignores their PR potential.

- **Rent it out.** Not feasible with a Board of Directors.
- **License it.** Not applicable.
- **Get rid of it.** As with anything, if it does not work - change it. A Board of Directors is too valuable and serious an asset to accept anything less than the best. Have the courage to ask unproductive Board Directors to leave.

## MEMBERSHIPS

Companies belong to all kinds of organizations such as trade associations, industrial associations, professional societies, chambers of commerce, international groups, charities, foundations, and other non-profits. These are valuable networks and a platform for creating and promoting the company's image.

- **Make it contribute.** Most companies have employees who belong to the various groups, participate in their events and may even be on their boards. What they lack, however, is a coordinated strategy for leveraging these relationships. What causes and considerations does your company want to promote in each of these entities?
- **Leverage it.** How can you leverage a membership? If all a membership does is cost you money and takes up your time, from a business standpoint, you are not getting your money's worth. Memberships can be leveraged to promote your brand, your company, and even your products and services. They are also a good source of information about the market, the competition and technology. In addition, if you serve on, or head up a committee, or even become president of the association, you establish a position in the industry. Further, along the way, you will inevitably meet people, who

are knowledgeable, interesting, and can become very helpful over the years. Consider this: the more visible you become outside your company, the more attention you draw to it.

- **Sell it.** Actually, some memberships can be sold, Country Club memberships, for instance. But while you cannot sell most business-related memberships, you can help recruit new members for those organizations, which gives you a chance to broaden your network even more. Every meeting you attend is another opportunity to promote your business, preferably without irritating people.
- **Rent it out.** Not applicable.
- **License it.** Not really, but there is always the possibility that you could help open new chapters in other locations, which again widens your network and offers more opportunities to get more business.
- **Get rid of it.** If you are not making any headway at achieving your objectives, then get rid of your membership.

## INVENTORIES

From a financial point of view, inventories are money that is just sitting there doing nothing. From a production and sales point of view, inventories take the pressure off of having to wait to meet orders. "Managing inventories" is challenging. On the one hand, the ideal situation would be to not have any inventory, and just ship production as it comes off the line. On the other hand, you want to be able to ship orders as soon as you get them without having to wait for production. How do you balance this?

Probably, the first place to look is at product lines. Do you really need as many as you have? Which are profitable, and which are not? Which of them are larger volume, which are not? Be careful about supplier volume discounts. Yes, you may get a better price if you buy more, but what good does it do you if it is just going to sit there and you have to pay for storage space? Which turn over faster? Which can you buy rather than produce? How can you speed up supplier delivery times? Can you get suppliers of finished products to ship directly to your customers? The number of issues that affect inventory management is almost endless, and each industry has a unique set of factors to consider, in addition to those directly related to your company's specific circumstances. One way or another, inventory must always be carefully scrutinized on a regular basis. There has been a whole industry created around Supply Chain Management.

- **Make it contribute.** What is your return on your investment in inventory? This may be hard to quantify, but perhaps you can measure it in terms of the value of benefits that you receive from your inventory. Of course, this raises the question of how valid is that value? If you list the top 10 of a specific product line's benefits from most to least valuable, and rate them on a 1 – 5 scale, with 5 being the best, you can compare the total for each product line. Then you can relate the outcome to the cost of that product line's inventory.

- **Leverage it.** For certain products where customers place high value on faster delivery, it may be possible to offer faster delivery for a small premium, which might justify maintaining a larger inventory. If you have products that carry different brand names, you might be able to store them without a label and apply it when they are ordered.

- **Sell it.** If a specific stock is moving too slowly, at what point does it begin to cost you too much to keep it stored? You may want to change it somehow to make it more attractive or decide to discontinue and sell-off the excess at a special price.

- **Rent it out.** Some types of equipment lend themselves to renting. In effect, this is what automotive companies do by leasing cars.

- **License it.** Not applicable.

- **Get rid of it.** If, you cannot sell it at a reduced price, consider donating it and getting a tax break.

Although they say that the definition of *Useful* is "something you gave away last week and now need it" rarely applies to businesses. On the contrary, make it a point to hold an ANNUAL "GET- RID OF IT" "CLEAN-UP" OPERATION where you ask all departments to review their assets and possessions with an eye to reducing what essentially is nothing but clutter, and also finding new ways to get greater benefit from all resources.

# CHAPTER NINE
# Going Global

## Your Future is Global

Performed well, Profit, Sales, Marketing, and Innovation, all add up to Growth. But what if there is not enough room to grow i.e. enough market? When you put a plant in a pot and water it regularly, it will grow, that is, *until it outgrows the pot and then begins to wilt.*

The pot you have planted your business in is your country. Most countries, including the USA, eventually reach a point where markets have become so competitive that growth becomes harder and harder to achieve as markets mature.

In this chapter, we are going to explore that larger pot called the Global Market and share specific approaches that can work for you. But first let's consider whether you are among those who may be *Starving in the Midst of Plenty!*

A scientist placed a number of small fish in an aquarium and left them there for a few days until they became acclimated. After herding all of them into one end, he separated the aquarium into two halves by placing a glass partition in the middle. He then placed a large predator fish in the other half.

Within seconds, the big fish spotted the little ones and dashed after them. Swimming at full speed, he smacked right into the glass partition. Stunned, he hesitated and hovered in one place for a few seconds. Recovering from the blow, he dashed toward the smaller ones again. Once more, he smashed into the glass partition.

In a near frenzy, the predator assaulted the invisible barrier time and again. Finally, reality sank in and he gave up. After a while, he swam around his half of the tank ignoring the smaller fish at the other end.

A few hours later, the scientist removed the glass partition. The large fish continued to swim around his half of the aquarium and never once attempted to cross to the other side. He would have starved to death in the midst of plenty had the scientist not returned him to another tank where he was fed regularly.

## LESSONS

1. You can starve in the midst of plenty.
2. Circumstances change.
3. Obstacles are rarely permanent, but not trying can make them immovable.
4. Your mind is the only limit to the size of your market.
5. Don't quit. Stay the course.

American companies all too often abandon foreign markets as soon as they become difficult. Then, a few years later, when they decide to return, local consumers remember how they were left stranded, and reject the product or service.

## GLOBAL MARKET, THE BIGGEST FISH TANK

Today, the biggest fish tank of them all is the Global Market. It is virtually without limit, filled with opportunities swimming around waiting to be gobbled up. The question is: "But gobbled up by whom?"

Abraham Lincoln is credited with saying: "All things come to those who wait, *but they come sooner to those who hustle!*" Time continues to prove him right.

I believe that if you want to grow revenues and profits faster than US markets allow, you must go global. Consider this: 96 *percent of the world's population lives outside the United States.* Not all of that population may be the right consumers for your products and services, but when you realize that the total global population is over 6 billion, it still leaves a lot to choose from.

Further, when you look at the largest leading companies in the Fortune 500, most of them derive more than 50 percent of their revenues and profits from international markets. Granted, these are huge companies, but they did not start that way. Whatever the size of your business, the global market has much to offer and, although you may not realize it, you have a lot to offer to them too.

Look at it this way, not all potential revenue streams are in your own country. That is why many companies are in international markets, or thinking of getting into them. When they do, after a while, certain patterns emerge.

**Don't Back into the Global Market.**

Many companies seem to back into global markets rather than advance into them. If a company has a good product or service, sooner or later it will become known beyond the domestic market. In time, it is bound to receive inquiries from potential buyers in other countries. These inquiries are what I call "Over the transom business." Somebody throws it at the company. There is no effort involved in developing it.

Most companies are geared for domestic business. When international business shows up, they often don't know what to do with it. As a client of mine says, "It's like dating a mermaid. She's in the water and you're on land. What do you do?"

*I suppose the answer to that one is: "You learn to swim."*

I know of companies that consider international business too much trouble. Perhaps, the amount of the initial sale may not be large enough to be appealing. Although that may be true - for the individual sale - the first time, it is a short-sighted view.

## A WRONG WAY TO APPROACH INTERNATIONAL BUSINESS

- Typically, an inquiry arrives from a foreign country, and offers the possibility of a new market. Because the company lacks international experience and interest, what might have been considered an opportunity had the inquiry been from a U.S. source, in this case it becomes a problem, almost a nuisance. There is no procedure in that company for handling international business.

- Not having any other source of information (and not looking for one), the sales manager says,
- 'Let's double our price and demand an upfront payment, and see what happens. That ought to take care of it." Imagine his surprise when he later gets an order with a check included for the amount quoted. He finally figures out how to handle it, and the order ships.
- Sometime later, another order from the same source also arrives with a check. Surprisingly, month after month, the orders keep on coming. The sales manager is delighted, but does nothing to pursue the matter further. He never finds out how the foreign client can afford to pay twice the price, nor is he particularly interested in learning how the product is being used or distributed in that country.
- The pattern continues. Eventually, an on-going relationship is established and, at one point, the client announces he will visit the company. He is well received, given a tour of the plant, taken to lunch, exchanges business cards, and suggests broadening the relationship to a next stage such as an official representation or distributorship.
- The company, without any further investigation or research, agrees. After all, it makes sense - in principle. A known customer with a good record, and a chance to break into a new market with little effort; why not?

Actually, there can be many reasons for not jumping into a commitment that, in effect, turns over an entire market to one individual or company in the area.

- What is the client doing in that market?

- What kind of reputation does he have in his country?
- Is the company's product being sold properly?
- Many companies that got started in international business this way later discovered they were in the wrong country, with the wrong distributor, and did not have a solid representation there.

Well, there may be a lot of "Not's" that need looking at. But the basic point is: a little planning and strategizing in advance of international commitments can save a lot of headaches later on. This is not hard to do, but it does take some discipline - mostly restraint and some analysis.

There are two more points I would like to stress:

1. When you begin to think about your international business, don't think small. My experience has been that most companies make mistakes because they think too small.
2. It is okay to start small, but don't think small. Set big, long term goals, but do your homework first.

## A MATTER OF PERCEPTION

A lot is in how you look at things. There is a story that's been around for quite a few years about two shoe salesmen sent to a Third World African country (talk about tough territories). One salesman sends e-mails back to his office: "Returning home. No prospects of sales. Natives don't wear shoes." The other salesman has a different perception and sends the following wire: "Send all possible stock. We can dominate the market. Natives don't wear shoes." When you look for opportunity, you are more likely to find it.

## Global Challenges and Opportunities Presented by Changing Times

We hear and read a lot about climate change, and it is important, but so is the change that is taking place in the business world. The following factors are for your consideration. You may want to discuss each of the challenges with your team to determine how exactly it will, or could affect, your business. As *you go through them, keep in mind that challenges hide opportunities.*

- **Challenge.** Supply exceeds demand for the first time in human history, especially in manufacturing. **Opportunity.** If you are in manufacturing, global competition is still growing, chances are you might have some uniqueness that is not yet global, which would give you an edge in a number of foreign markets. And, if you are innovative, the whole world is now demanding new products and concepts.
- **Challenge.** Quality is a given, and today's consumers are quick to abandon suppliers whose quality does not stand up to expectations. **Opportunity.** If quality is one of your strengths, you have an advantage.
- **Challenge.** For every product/service there is an equal and opposite product/service somewhere. In business, uniqueness tends to fade quickly. **Opportunity.** All the more reason to get out there before your uniqueness fades and keep up your R&D.
- **Challenge.** You will be underpriced consistently. No matter how low your prices, someone will always offer a lower one. **Opportunity.** That is why the perception of value that you create will open global doors for you.
- **Challenge.** Most products and services are look-alikes. Commoditization is a global factor. **Opportunity.** The more you can differentiate your product and your service, the more money you can make everywhere.

- **Challenge.** Borderless markets invite competition. The more markets open, the more competition. **Opportunity.** But, while it is a mistake to underestimate local competition, local markets are always open to new and different offerings that match their need, wants, and preferences from a cultural point of view.
- **Challenge.** Telecommunications level the playing field; they have substantially increased information and reduced lead times. **Opportunity.** This works in your favor if you can use all media effectively.
- **Challenge.** Lowest price is no longer sustainable because, as the global economy grows raw materials and ingredients will become scarcer and more costly, thus raising production costs. China is already heading that direction. **Opportunity.** This means that even though your costs and your prices may be higher than local ones abroad, low price strategies are weakening everywhere, which opens the door for your products and services.
- **Challenge.** Business growth is increasingly difficult, especially in the United States where our markets are maturing and competition is more aggressive and sophisticated. **Opportunity.** All the more reason to think and act global.
- **Challenge.** Foreign competition is not always obvious because it can be part of a domestic product or carry an English brand name. **Opportunity.** On the other hand, you can now make your products and technology parts of foreign companies' products and services.
- **Challenge.** Businesses everywhere must now FIGHT to stay in business as the rollercoaster of economic cycles have become more frequent and impactful, which also increases the intensity of competition. **Opportunity.** But, having survived in the American market of recent years gives you a sophisticated edge for competing in other markets – as long as you can adapt it to local cultures and preferences.

If you go about it right way, **your international business should equal or surpass your domestic business in ten years or less!** I would like to encourage you to keep that thought in mind.

Make the most of this information:

- Set a specific goal
- Establish a timeline
- Think ACTION!

Everywhere around the world competitors are starving *for your job and your business! A little paranoia can be a healthy thing! Time to Fight Back!* If foreign competitors have learned how to penetrate and thrive in your markets, you can do the same in theirs.

**The rewards can be gigantic -- if you keep at it and learn along the way!**

**A thought for you to consider: There may be global brands, but there is no such thing as a global customer. CUSTOMERS EVERYWHERE ARE LOCAL! Your product or service will do well provided you take into account local cultures and preferences.**

1. Accelerate and increase your global business. Identify the key characteristics of different cultures
2. And successfully adapt your approach to the preferences of local markets.

As you are on the Internet, you're already global, so you had better begin to think globally. In so doing, it is important to think big, but start small. Here are some suggestions:

- Design an easy-to-scan website. Internet attention spans are incredibly short.
- Offer FREE Information (Useful Info). People appreciate truly useful information that helps them make better purchasing decisions.

- Research your overseas target customer groups. Just because they are in the same group doesn't mean they are the same.

You probably have more to sell than you realize. Remember the Sausage Machine where you put a pig in one end and sausages come out the other? They say it uses everything but the squeal. Take a hard look at your business in terms of what you may have to offer that you do not even realize.

## What Do You Have to Offer?

The following checklist outlines some of the saleable items you may not have considered saleable.

The four main categories are:
- Products
- Reputation
- Service
- Know-how

## Products

Here are some of the areas related to product where you may be able to build sales.

- **Product lines.** Every product line is probably saleable around the world. You can sell the products individually, or the product line itself to someone else to sell in their country.
- **Raw materials.** Not all raw materials are easy to get in all countries. You could enter into an alliance with one of your suppliers to help them sell in other countries.
- **Components.** Some of the components you make for or use in your own product may be saleable to producers of similar products in other countries.

- **Sub-assemblies.** Either you can offer the same as recommended for components, or you could assemble different ones for foreign manufacturers.
- **Designs.** Your designs may be attractive to foreign companies.
- **Fashion.** If you are in a business where fashion is a key element, its attraction tends to be global. Fashion relates to credibility. Once established, it is very saleable such as brands as Gucci and other European names.
- **Packaging.** I see so many highly creative packaging solutions in the everyday products that we all use that could solve lots of problems around the world. A company in Chicago, Magenta, designs and produces amazing enclosures to solve unique customer packaging needs. They could license their patents overseas.
- **Uses.** How many uses do customers create for your products? Many companies are not aware of the many different ways customers use their products. For example, amateur gardeners tear strips of pantyhose to tie plants. It is strong and elastic, better than many of the special products sold for that specific use. Different end-uses can become niches everywhere in the world.
- **Your Supply Chain.** Check your supply chain. Each of your suppliers could either become a potential partner in an overseas venture or could be a piggy-back distributor of your products.

## REPUTATION

It takes years to establish a worthy reputation in your industry or field of activity. Why waste it on just one market?

- **Brands.** Brands can be incredibly powerful in global markets. The Asians realize this and that is why they are trying so hard to create worldwide brands that can open markets for themselves. Once you establish a brand in the United States, it likely has credibility in other countries.

- **Labels.** Creative, stylish, label designs add to the power of most products. If your products owe much of their success to the quality of their labels, it will make your products much more attractive to buyers in other markets.
- **Logos.** Good logos achieve immediate recognition. Attractive logos could open doors around the world to your products and services.

## SERVICE

One of the major weaknesses of companies around the world is service, but those companies that excel in this area are valued by customers everywhere. You would think it would be easy to develop systems and policies that ensure quality service but, apparently, most companies are too busy with other functions to pay attention to this real customer value. Whether or not you would be interested in using your own customer service systems and procedures for opening foreign markets, make it a point for your company to become a role model for great *service and you will sustainably grow your profits.*

- **Customer service systems and procedures.** I do not know if Nordstrom uses its customer service systems and procedures to open foreign markets, but they are so good that they definitely could.
- **Service to the foreign buyer.** Most U.S. companies seem not to even think of the need for outstanding service when dealing with foreign buyers. This could be a door opener if you focused on it.
- **Service to the foreign buyer's customers.** Take it a step beyond your foreign customer to his or her customers in that country or in this one. What service could you provide in either case?

- **Servicing equipment.** Depending on the nature of the products you sell overseas, if it involves equipment and or technology, service will be needed sooner or later. When selling products overseas give thought in advance to how to provide saleable services.
- **Repairs.** In many countries where equipment and technology are sold, there is not much in the way of certified repair services; this could offer profitable possibilities.
- **Testing.** If you test in the U.S., you could do it overseas. With today's communication and video technology, even surgery is being offered at a distance. Many foreign countries cannot afford the level of testing equipment that they might need; if you could find a way to help solve this problem from a distance, you will have opened up a whole new market.
- **Parts.** If you use them, most likely so do foreign companies. If your relationships with the suppliers of those parts are good, you could actually sell them yourself and your supplier would be delighted to help you do so.
- **Purchasing services.** Equal industries and businesses usually need to buy the same things, but many foreign companies face substantial difficulties with their purchasing efforts. You could offer to make the purchases for those companies. This is a type of outsourcing except that this one finds products from the U.S. for foreign buyers.
- **Distribution.** Your distribution setup may offer the potential for providing distribution for foreign products in the U.S. If you already have distribution in some countries, not all overseas companies may have representation in those countries; you could offer this service.
- **Financing.** This one is a little more complex, but basically you could find sources that would help the foreign buyers of your products finance their purchases.
- **Consulting.** Your company's expertise is valuable and could

be provided to customers in other countries, or even licensed to them.

## Know-How

As mentioned above, your expertise is valuable. Each of the areas presented below is often a challenge for companies in other countries. Your expertise in your specific industry could be extremely helpful to foreign companies in the same industry. Not only could you provide consulting but also training, which opens up a whole new market.

- Technology
- Specifications
- Standards
- Ratios
- Procedures
- Information Systems
- Engineering
- Design
- Sourcing
- Training
- Processes
- Manufacturing
- Assembly
- Research and Development
- Legal
- Marketing
- Advertising
- Promotion
- Strategic Planning
- Management

If you use this list to analyze your business from the point of view of what you might have to offer in the global market, you are bound to find a number of potential new revenue streams that can substantially enhance your Profit.

**Question.** The above is what you have to offer. The next question is what do the various countries have to offer you?

## 33 QUESTIONS YOU SHOULD ASK BEFORE YOU GROW YOUR BUSINESS INTERNATIONALLY

What do you need to know before you choose a specific country? These questions will help you grow your profits and avoid costly mistakes.

What You Need to Know Questionnaire. 33 questions to help you plan ahead

1. Who would be the typical users of your products in other countries?
2. What is their income?
3. How are such products priced in those countries?
4. Will your target consumers be able to afford your products?
5. What are the similarities between your products and locally available ones?
6. What are the differences?
7. Do people use them the same way?
8. Are sizes different?
9. What are the local preferences?
10. Is the same type of packaging practical?
11. Are there any social/cultural nuances related to the use of your products?
12. How are such products supplied in other countries?
13. Are there local producers of similar products? How do they compare?
14. Is the market price-oriented?

15. Who are your competitors in those markets?
16. How good are they? How well established?
17. What kinds and how much support would your products require to sell?
18. What is the typical distribution pattern in those markets?
19. What are the usual payment terms in those markets?
20. Is local financing available to you?
21. Is it available to your target distributors?
22. What would the logistics of supplying those markets involve?
23. What are the customs duties on your product if you decide to ship it into those markets?
24. If you decided to manufacture locally, would all the ingredients or components be available?
25. What are the health and consumer protection requirements of those markets?
26. What are the legal liabilities of product failure?
27. Would you need to position your product or your brand differently? How?
28. Has anyone registered your brand or a similar one in those markets?
29. Do the nations of those markets allow repatriation of profits?
30. What are the local labor laws?
31. Would you need to change your marketing approach?
32. Would you be allowed to use the same advertising slogans and materials as in your home market?
33. How will you monitor the sale of your products?

If you are a potential exporter and marketer of goods and services, the above questions will help you better prepare for entry into foreign markets.

Finally, as your share of global business grows so will the complexity of managing it. Eventually, you may end up with operations in various countries managed by either American expatriates or senior local executives. At this point, your leadership will involve aspects that are not common to managing in the United States, and you will be entering the field of The Global Executive, a whole new and very complex leadership role.

## TOP GLOBAL LEADERS HAVE TO BE THE BEST TEAM-BUILDERS

---

*But of a good leader, who talks little, and when his work is done, his aim fulfilled, they will all say, "We did it ourselves."*
Lao Tzu (500 BC)

---

**Running a global operation with managers in many different countries is like trying to drive a car from the back seat.** You do not have the view and the perspective, nor do you have the controls that those in the front seat, the on-site managers, have. Yet, if you manage international operations, you are responsible for what happens throughout the company's global operations. It is a tough job, but nobody in your organization knows just how tough it really is.

The only way that you can survive is by creating a truly exceptional global leadership team that runs by itself while coordinating with you and each of the other team members.

You may be the boss according to the organization chart but, if you do things right, you will be a member of an exceptional team that also does the right things right and makes you look great. And, because it takes a team to win, you will also win.

- **Multicultural team building – Key to global leadership.**
  "How do I manage twelve managers in twelve different countries?" asks the President of the International Division of a Fortune 500 company. The answer is: You Do Not. You build a team, and they manage with you! Effective multi-national teams are the key to the success of today's best global

businesses such as Coca-Cola, Hewlett Packard, and many others,

- **Multi-cultural teams tend to be more successful in global marketing.** Teams of self-directed, multi-cultural managers often solve not only their problems, but also each-others and sometimes – even their bosses. They are quicker to understand and respond to the complex demands of today's fast-paced, highly competitive global markets.
- **The best teams get member buy-in on goals and objectives.** You get team members to agree on goals: give them room to act, get out of their way, and *watch them eat your competition's lunch.* Top performers want to have a sense of being in control of their own destiny. They tend to reject anything they perceive as imposed from on high. What they *help* to plan, they feel they *own.* The best leaders consult more than order. **The best global leaders create a team mystique.** They constantly sell the qualities of team members to one another, creating a mystique that motivates them to work together. They encourage team members to consult with one another. International Operations executives who try to do everything themselves become bottlenecks, frustrate everyone, and wear themselves out.
- **Each member of the team gets to host a team meeting in their country.** This relieves the leader of the burden of organizing such meetings. It enhances the status of the host and also creates opportunities for social interaction between team members.
- **They create task forces among the team members.** Top leaders leverage strengths of individual team members on special projects that benefit all. They also help them understudy one another. This is cross-training and teambuilding at its best!
- **They work as Virtual Teams linked by telephone, internet and video conferencing.** They keep a steady flow of

conversation between the team members and themselves. The worst thing you can do is keep a team in the dark.

- **They represent and coach team members on career issues.** Being away from headquarters can sometimes have a negative effect on an executive's career. Great global leaders recognize this and work hard to engineer members career progress.
- **They get to know each member's family.** Enlightened global leaders show they care. They know family welfare is essential to key executive performance, especially with ex-pats.
- **Great global team leaders relinquish leadership to team members as needed.** Self-confident leaders are willing to accept their limitations. When one team member has belter knowledge in a given area, the leader looks to him or her to guide the whole team in that area. *A true leader does not always need to be a boss to be in command.*

## Successful Global Leaders Make Leaders of All Team Members. The Result?

### OUTSTANDING PERFORMANCE!

As the level of globalization continues to grow, the nature of teams is becoming more multi-cultural, both in the United States and abroad. While this section covers team building from a global perspective, the concepts and principle involved are also applicable to U.S. operations.

It is estimated that about 75 percent of employees sent to work and live overseas, fail. Why? Because they are improperly selected. Companies assume that success in the U.S. guarantees success abroad. It does not, and the numbers prove it.

Yet, U.S. companies still don't get it. They keep sending the wrong people overseas who end up producing a huge negative ROI. How much? Check the following figures.

- On an average, sending an employee to a foreign country costs American companies about $300,000 a year.
- Assume a company sends just 17 employees abroad in a given year. The annual cost of those 17 employees is about $5,100,000.
- The average overseas assignment lasts about 4 years.
- The cost of keeping 17 employees overseas for 4 years is $20,400,000.
- If 75 percent or 13 of those 17 employees fail, the negative ROI is $15,300,000.
- Further, the cost of the mistakes that improperly selected employees make during their stay abroad may equal, double, triple or more, than just the cost of their compensation.

U.S. companies send thousands of employees overseas every year. Given the outrageous cost of these poor decisions, companies should invest more time and money up front to choose the right candidates. They should also track the cost of sending those wrong candidates overseas.

Yet, regardless of the size of your business, today it is more important than ever to go global. Here's why:

- The U.S. government is printing money at the rate of more than $11 billion a day!
- Flooding the world with dollars has lowered their value.
- In 1999, the Euro was worth only $0.85 dollars. At the time of the publishing of this book, it is worth US $ 1.18.
- U.S. markets are shrinking, which makes it much harder to grow a business.
- Conclusion: you need to find new markets. Where? Go global!

BUT - before going global, do your homework! Analyze and study the country, the market, and the culture that you have chosen as a target. Make no assumptions about other countries, markets, and cultures, based strictly on U.S. experience. Once you have defined the nature of the people in the target country, ask yourself what kind of persons should you select to work with them?

## 20 KEY QUESTIONS YOU NEED TO ASK OF POTENTIAL EXPATS

- Have they ever lived, or at least traveled, overseas?
- Are they set in their ways?
- Do they adjust easily to new circumstances?
- Are they people-friendly?
- Do they speak any other languages?
- Are they capable of learning enough of the required language before going there?
- Are their personal/family needs such that they can only be met in the United States?
- Are they insightful managers and leaders?
- Will their spouses and children be able to adjust to the new environment?
- Can they stand the initial isolation that goes with being a foreigner in another country?
- Are they resourceful?
- Are they good negotiators?
- Can they adapt and yet not go entirely native?
- Are they good communicators?
- Will their leadership style match the nature of local employees?
- Are they good decision makers?
- Do they know anything about the target country?
- Do they have any habits or weaknesses that could get them in trouble?
- Do they have the indispensable "street smarts" to navigate safely in a strange environment?
- Are they good networkers?

There are more wrong kinds of people to send abroad than right ones. The right ones build relationships. Wherever you go in the world, building relationships is the key to business. Business is about people, and not everyone is right for every country, market, and culture. So, *if you want to be profitable, be sure to analyze candidates carefully, and choose only after extensive interviewing and reviewing.*

You don't become an expert in international business overnight, but unless you get started you can't even begin to develop the expertise you will need for success in the global market. This chapter gets you started, but nothing teaches better than actual experience. If you feel somewhat uncertain, then it may be to your benefit to consult some of the many services listed below.

If you are already in the global market, these same sources will help you to develop both a more in-depth knowledge and a broader view that will open your eyes to more and greater opportunities.

## How to Research Foreign Markets

How do you get information about markets in other countries? What kind of research do you need? Will it be very expensive? Will it be enough?

- **What to look for.** Basically, you are trying to find out if a market may exist for your product or service, and what it may take to penetrate it.
- **Where to look.** Start locally and use as many sources as you can.
- **Internet your way to data.** Hoover Online. Google. Foreign country websites. Chat rooms.
- **Inexpensive Research.** The United States Department of Commerce has an abundance of information about overseas markets and how to access them.
- The Senate and House Foreign Relations Committees.

- **The CIA** has an excellent database that is open to all.
- **Your state government** probably has a department of commerce with an international section.
- **Your local library** is a gold mine of information sources (be sure to talk with the Reference Librarian).
- **The trade missions** of foreign countries have offices in many U.S. cities.
- Local offices of foreign consulates.
- **United States Commercial Service Websites** to remember: www.export.gov, and www.BuyUSA.com.
- U.S. Commercial Services phone number: 1-800-USA-TRAD(E)

Other handy websites:

- www.sba.gov/financing/frinternational.html
- www.usatrade.gov
- www.exim.gov
- www.tda.gov Trade & Development Agency www.bxa.gov Bureau of ExportAdministration
- www.tradematch.co.uk Helps to match companies with overseas potential partners. Fill out a form and they will do the tracking for you.
- www.traderoots.org US Chamber of Commerce. On their website, look up their international division which lists the addresses of all the AMCHAMS (American Chambers, overseas chapters of the U.S. Chamber of Commerce, an excellent resource of regional information)
- www.aacla.org American Association of Chambers in Latin America www.wayp.com International Yellow Pages www.yellowpages.com
- www.globalyp.com/world.htm

## Some Closing Thoughts:

With regard to going global, please consider the following:

The current population of the United States is 331 million.

The world population is 7.6 billion

96 percent of that population lives **outside** the United States.

That means 7.3 billion potential customers who would like to live a better life that you can contribute to with your products and services.

*Important Question. Wouldn't you like to help those 7.3 billion people live a better life and also grow your sales and profits at the same time?*

# CHAPTER TEN
# It Takes a Team to Win

## People Power Pays!

---

*"In the end, all business operations can be reduced to*
*three words; people, product and profits.*
*Unless you've got a good team,*
*you can't do much with the other two."*
Lee Iacocca

---

In the 1980 Winter Olympics at Lake Placid, NY, the American hockey team, composed mostly of college students, defeated the Soviet team, reputed be the best hockey team in the world, and composed mainly of professional players. Why did the American team win? There are several lessons that can be learned from this event:

1.  The Soviets may have been overconfident, and they obviously underestimated the potential of the American team.
2.  The American players were typical of the American culture in that they did not think they could not win.
3.  The Soviets expected the Americans to use standard strategies and moves. Instead, the Americans did the unexpected and tried all kinds of unconventional plays and moves.
4.  The Soviet team was composed mainly of individual star players who not only were good, but also believed that they were. In sports, as in many other endeavors, stars tend to be more focused on themselves than on the team. They are

eager to shine individually which often means they do not work well with the other players.

5. The American team was a true team in the sense that they all had the same objective: to win. They shared the same interests, the same mutual respect, helped one another, supported one another, and behaved like the Three Musketeers in that they were "All for One and One for All". Not only that, but on a true team everyone can be the leader at a given moment when their skills and knowledge are the best for that specific situation.

6. Further, it is not the team with the best players that wins, but the team that plays the best as a team that day, as the Americans did, and not as the bunch of unfocused stars as the Soviets did.

## In the Corporate World, Why Does It Take a Team to Win?

The best answer to that question is that hierarchy does not guarantee success. Just because someone has a high-level job does not mean that they will be successful. There is no one person, no matter how talented, who can do everything, find the time to do it, and do it well. If anyone thinks that all they need is a group of subordinates who report to them and will follow orders, not only are they wrong, but in the wrong time period. The day of Command and Order is no longer around, and it never worked anyway. Further, in todays' global 24/7 world, life and business are far more complicated than ever before.

If people are the key to Profit, then not only do we need good people working with us (you will notice I said "with" not "for" us), but we need to know how to work with them (rather than "on" them). Smart capable people are, and should be, self-driven and self-managed initiators who lead more than follow, and strive for excellence and exceptional results – provided that you, their leader, share a worthy and motivating vision with them and lead by example.

Will they always agree with you? No! Once you convince them of the value of the goal, they will commit to it with everything they have, and do their best to ensure your success. This kind of team requires a steady stream of meaningful communication but will not absorb a lot of your time. Once you point the direction, they will be off and running.

## COMMITTEE VERSUS TEAM

It is important that you know the difference between a team and a committee. On a committee, every one represents a different interest. As stated above, on a team, everyone shares the same interests, the same goals, and the same commitment. They respect one another, believe in one another, support and help one another, and their motto is the same as that of The Three Musketeers, "One for all and all for one" (Sorry, but if you didn't see any of the 10 or so movies about the Three Musketeers, you'll have to read the book)

To keep a team winning there needs to be a leader, but each member gets to lead when his or her expertise is superior to that of the appointed leader for that specific situation. As mentioned earlier, the only constant in business is change. To keep the team winning, the mission of all leaders becomes *to help their teams to successfully cope with change.*

**The true change leader must be able to see the invisible and deliver the impossible.**

To do so, the leader must develop a *Team Building Culture.*

## DEVELOPING A TEAM BUILDING CULTURE

Culture is defined as the values and beliefs that an organization encourages, adheres to and rewards. A team-building culture encourages leadership, collaboration, and respect, and empowers its members to make their own decisions appropriately.

Ideally, at every level within an organization, there will be teams dedicated to making the company grow and be more profitable. Winning teams are functional and cross functional.

Functional teams operate at several levels within each of the departmental areas such as manufacturing, product development, finance, human resources, technology, sales and marketing, maintenance, engineering, and administration. They help each function to excel in its area of expertise by delivering the results specified within the strategic plan thus fulfilling the company mission.

Since no teams other than the top executive team and the board of directors, oversee the total company, at each level of functional teams there will be a need for cross-functional teams that bring together the different types of expertise to deliver well-rounded results. This reduces the tendency of departments and divisions to become independent silo republics.

In successful organizations, the leaders at each level constantly stress the fact that the company is one big team with multiple levels that help the entire organization meet the short, and long term, goals.

The culture of the teams at the top will be different than that of those at lower levels, but they too must be aligned with, and respect, one another, and focused on the same vision and mission. Those at the top may have a broader vision of the business, but those at the lower level are closer to the specifics that convert that vision into reality.

Leaders also help all participants to understand that the purpose of every employee's work is, to deliver value and delight to customers while making a worthy profit. The focus needs to be not on you or even your teams, but on the customers you bring products and services to, and how you can better serve them.

This kind of mentality helps everyone to view the entire organization as a team with a shared mission and a vision. It fosters inclusion and cooperation rather than isolation and exclusion.

When teams are bottom line focused, but also people sensitive and motivated to serve customer needs, the customers will develop emotional ties with the team members they deal with. Result? *The company will be profitable.* Employees will feel purposeful and productive, which gives them a sense of accomplishment.

In companies where this does not happen, employees usually feel unfulfilled and miserable. Result? *Miserable employees produce miserable customers which produces miserable profits.*

## TEAM CULTURE-BASED RECRUITMENT

While companies are not military organizations, they can certainly learn from them. The Navy Seals Special Ops Teams approach to team building is a good example. The selection process is very rigorous, and for good reason, because these are teams that will be sent on critically important and dangerous missions. The team members are true believers, committed to their team and its mission, hardworking, disciplined, highly knowledgeable, yet versatile and dedicated to excellence.

A business cannot and would not put its recruitment candidates through a similar environment and process as the Navy Seals employ, but it can learn the importance and value of well-planned and carefully executed candidate selection.

All too often, company employee selection process is more focused on the experience, and the technical and educational qualifications of candidates rather than their character, energy, collaborative skills, ethics, reasoning, decision making, and creative capacity. The screening may be done either by a search firm or by the human resources staff. Once candidates pass this screening, they are interviewed by two or three experienced executives who may, or may not, be good interviewers, and a decision is made.

This process may seem logical, but it is too quick. To begin with, it often uses the job title and responsibilities as the key elements of the search. Businesses should devote more time to analyzing the nature of the job and the related requirements. They also need to identify the qualifications and personal characteristics that relate to the special challenges that await the candidate immediately upon arrival. Plus, down the road, they also need to define the company's specific performance expectations.

Of course, interviews are important to get a feeling for the human aspect of the candidate, but they should go way beyond just reviewing the resume and job history. *If there was ever a time for a 360 degrees evaluation, this is it.* The people who will work with the candidate, both superiors and subordinates, should be given an opportunity to form and share their impressions too.

Lots of questions can be asked.

- What did you not like about the place where you worked before?
- What would it have taken for you to stay there?
- What different things would you like to see in our company?
- -Is there anything about our company and its culture that might make you uncomfortable?
- How would you describe your management style?
- How would the people who worked with you describe it?
- What kind of management style would you prefer from your boss?
- What are your pet peeves? Why?
- What do you think of your previous bosses?
- What did they do right?
- What did they do wrong?
- What kind of boss have you worked best with?
- What are you good at?
- What things do you need to thrive in your job?
- What things are more challenging/frustrating for you?
- What are some of the key lessons you have learned along the way?
- What was your favorite sport in school?
- What are your hobbies?
- What was the most difficult assignment you ever had?

- Have you ever had to fire someone? What was that experience like?
- What do you look for in the people who report to you?
- What do you do to motivate people?
- What was your favorite subject in school?
- Did you ever serve in the military? Which branch?
- What lessons did you come away with?
- Did you have any jobs when you were in high school or college? What kind?
- Describe when you've led people through some change.

These are just some of the questions that might help bring to light more about the candidate's character and values.

It is usually a good idea to also give candidates a tour of the place where they will be working, meet some of the people and observe their reactions. If the location involves a manufacturing facility, even though their jobs may not be directly related to production, it can be interesting to observe how they see it, what they comment on, and get their opinions at the end of the tour. Along the way, you also can observe how they interact with the people they meet.

Every step of the recruiting, selecting, and interviewing should be a form of evaluation based on the final objective of the process: finding someone who will be a highly motivated and excellent team member, and who will also contribute strongly to the company mission and its bottom line.

Achieving this goal is not easy, and it is often necessary to continue monitoring the commitment of recently hired employees. Tony Hsieh, CEO of Zappos, the very successful Internet shoe retailer, places special emphasis on the importance of hiring employees who truly believe in the company's mission, which is to provide service that awes customers. His strategy for determining this commitment is to put new hires through a four-week training program, and then make them the following offer: if any of them want to quit at the end of the training period, they will be paid for the full time that they have ben in the training program, and will also receive a $1,000 bonus. So far, only 10 percent have accepted and left. The true believers who stay contributing to making Zappos employee retention rate and level of profit among the highest in that industry. Obviously, that investment in quality of hiring has paid off greatly.

**Note Again.** It is not the team with the best players that always wins, *but rather the team that plays the best that day!*

## TAKE COMMAND OF YOUR LEADER SHIP (BUT NOT THE TITANIC)

Ever wanted to be the captain of a ship? Whether you are running an entire company or a division or a department, your situation is similar to that of a ship's captain. That is why this chapter is referred to as The Leader Ship where the captain is the leader and the crew is the team.

- The captain sets the destination, oversees the navigation, and monitors the operations. Each member of the crew knows his or her job and how it relates to the mission of the ship. Officers direct and guide crew members in their performance. In the Navy, they say 'A clean ship is a good ship, and everyone tries to keep it that way'. Running a clean operation of any kind requires true leadership.
- Under normal circumstances, ships usually run smoothly. But normal circumstances are rarely common. High seas can create damage and chaos, equipment may not always perform reliably, supplies may run out and, from time to time, crew members may get sick or injured. In war time, the ship may have all of these and other problems, plus combat missions and the threat of enemy attacks.
- The captain is responsible for the welfare of the crew, for the performance of the ship, and the fulfillment of its mission.

The unexpected is not usually an acceptable excuse for poor performance; on the contrary, it is the captain's responsibility to expect and overcome the unexpected. Further, operations run 24/7 as is the case in the business world nowadays only more likely to be exercised.

- Now, ask yourself how much of a captain's job sounds a lot like yours (minus the ship, of course). You are responsible for fulfilling the mission of your job, reaching the pertinent goals on time and as planned, seeing to it that the people who report to you are properly prepared, equipped, and supervised and checking to see that they are indeed performing as required. While you are not responsible for the welfare of your subordinates, in a sense you are because you must be aware of their condition as it relates to their performance and safety.

- The business seas may be rough at times but, as Captain of the USS Business Leader Ship, you cannot afford to get the business equivalent of seasickness, at least not publicly. Why, because perception is often more important than reality. The leader is looked to as a role model. As a leader in the business world, you cannot afford to look weak, out of control, mean, dishonest, volatile, confused, panicky, afraid, sloppy or stupid. However, you can get sick because developing a sickness is generally viewed as beyond our control.

- So, if you cannot be perceived that way, how should you be perceived? The opinions regarding how a leader should be viewed vary with each person, the times, the organization, the situation, the gender, and the expectations of those who report to him or her as well as the expectations of those to whom the leader reports.

- We all report to someone and, although the sign on Harry Truman's desk said, "The buck stops here", even the president reports to the people and to God. But, if you want to come up with a list of characteristics of great leaders, then why not learn from them? Be aware, however, that great leaders were not and are not necessarily perfect human beings. Their merit lies in having achieved the distinction of being great leaders despite their imperfections as human beings.

## Leadership Qualities

There are many qualities that describe the different types of leaders but continuing with our concept of taking command of your leader ship, here are some of the characteristics of effective leaders in business and other areas.

- **Responsibility.** Leaders feel a responsibility to their followers, employees, superiors, customers, and the communities in which their organizations operate. That responsibility focuses on bringing better solutions to all, whether it be superior products and service to customers, greater returns to investors and stockholders, enabling employees to develop their potential, or contributing to the welfare of the communities where they work.
- **Accountability.** Leaders know who and how much they owe to, and hold themselves accountable for delivering on their promises and commitments.
- **Independence of Thought.** Great leaders may seek consensus but still follow their own vision of the best solution.
- **In-the-Trenches Experience.** Leaders have walked in the shoes of their followers and customers. They have lived first-hand the joys and pains of those they lead.
- **Clarity of Vision.** Great leaders convey very clear visions and goals that inspire and motivate others. Clarity, of course, has to begin with the leaders who must think through their intentions and expectations carefully before sharing them with others.
- **Action-Focused.** Leaders get people to like and accept their ideas, but the real challenge is getting people to take action.

- **People-Sensitive.** If you want to get people to want to do what you want to get done, you must be sensitive to their needs, values, and emotions.
- **Passion.** Great leaders are true believers, hard-working plus totally committed and devoted to their causes. They are passionate about their goals and their values.
- **Authentic.** They are what they are, nothing phony, true to their mission.
- **Innovative.** No one ever achieved greatness without inventing new solutions to both new and old problems.

*Question. On a scale of 1(lowest) to 10 (best), rank yourself on each of these qualities then add up your scores. You don't have to share the outcome with anyone, but judge yourself on where you stand as a leader.*

In her book, *e-LEADERSHIP*, author and very experienced consultant Susan Annunzio, tells the story of a highly successful manager and outstanding leader at SBC (Southwestern Bell Corporation, now AT&T) who, in late 1997, turned around an operation that had been noted for its high absenteeism, low productivity, excessive overtime costs, and high overall costs.

Bobby Soules, a 30-year telecommunications veteran, quickly diagnosed the problem: the employees had almost zero input into the business. Soules began to consult with the employees, and even the unions, on how to improve operations.

An amazing thing happens when leaders show respect for the intelligence, experience, and knowledge of their followers; *they feel recognized and perceived as valuable!* And, as morale improves, so does performance.

The operation cut its costs by over $1,000,000, absenteeism stopped being a problem, and the unit's productivity soared. Not only that, but both subordinates and superiors absolutely loved him, his leadership style, and his contribution to the benefit of everyone – including customers (even though the latter may not have known what or who was behind the improved service they received).

When thinking of leadership, it might be a good idea to keep in mind the mantra of the Marine Corps: "There are no bad soldiers. There are only bad officers."

There are many stories of great leaders and their leadership styles, and there is much that we can learn from them. The great sea battles of history are filled with stories of ships' captains whose leadership qualities led them and their crews to become legendary heroes. Books ranging from the adventures of Ulysses in Homer's the Odyssey, to the US Naval records of heroes in the greatest sea battle of World War Two in the Philippines Leyte Gulf describe the inspiring leadership qualities of sea captains. My favorite, however, is a series of novels by C.S Forester which tell the stories of fictional Captain Horatio Hornblower whose qualities are based on those of real leaders.

One true leadership story that has always fascinated me is that of Alexander the Great of Greece, a warrior (not a sea captain) who actually conquered most of the known world of his time when he was in his early thirties.

Now, you might ask "What can we learn from a leader dating back to the fourth century B.C. that could possibly relate to the business world and Profit?" It has to do with perception and how it can be leveraged, but the lessons learned also apply to today's world, and especially to business. Read on.

## ALEXANDER THE GREAT OF MACEDONIA

One would suppose that as the son of Phillip, the great Macedonian king who conquered all of Greece, Alexander would have been a pampered prince. He wasn't. He made it a point to spend time with the troops, learn their ways, compete with them in their physical training, and to be on a par even with the most skilled. *Along the way, he earned the respect of his father's troops and became a warrior and a skilled leader who knew how to motivate other warriors.*

At age 13, Alexander asked his father to buy a certain stallion for him. The stallion was unruly. No one had been able to mount it. Phillip deemed the stallion too wild and dangerous for the boy. Instead, Alexander grabbed the stallion's reins, turned it around, leapt on its back, and astounded everyone by riding off in full control. When asked later by his father how he had accomplished that feat, Alexander explained that he had observed what all the adults had missed: the horse was frightened by its own shadow. By turning it around to face the sun, Alexander removed the problem. A leader must see the invisible to achieve the impossible. *Alexander always found his own solutions.*

Alexander made it a point to observe things firsthand and form his own judgments. Although he fought many battles, Alexander never used the same strategy twice. He knew that what one man could do, another could repeat, so he *constantly innovated.*

From his earliest youth Alexander had trained himself to do everything the troops did – only better. As an adult leader, he suffered whatever his troops did. When they walked, he walked. When they were hungry, so was he. On one occasion, after crossing an Egyptian desert to reach a river, Alexander let his entire army of some 10,000 men drink before he allowed himself to do so. In battle, he often led the charge himself. Proof of his valor is that he was wounded eight times. Alexander demanded much of his army, *but he led by example.*

After crossing over into Asia Minor, Alexander was confronted by local priests who brought before him the Gordian Knot, an intricate tangle of ropes. They said: prophesy held that only a man who could unravel the Gordian Knot, would be able to conquer the region. No one had been able to do so in the past. Alexander took one look at the knot, pulled out his sword and, with a single stroke, cut through it. *Alexander applied his own rules when necessary.*

Alexander led an army of 35,000 men against Darius the emperor of Persia, who fielded over 200,000 men. At the battle of Issus, Alexander positioned his army with its back to the sea;

his men had no choice but to win – and they did. *Alexander was undaunted by odds.*

Alexander had confidence in his men because he personally saw to it that they were properly trained. He made professionals out of them first. Then, he had them apply their skills by matching them against larger armies. *He challenged but trained first.*

Alexander conquered many lands. In each, he encouraged his men to marry local women, and to adapt many of the local customs. He made his men obey local laws, and often reinstated local authorities to run the regions. He personally paid homage to local gods, and also adopted those customs he believed made him acceptable to the local population. In Egypt, he became a Pharaoh, and even dressed like one because he knew better than to attempt to change centuries of ritual. *He knew acquisitions must blend in rather than be forced into new molds.*

Alexander encouraged trade among the conquered lands, and also with the cities of Greece. His first step in that direction was to unify the currencies of all his lands. *He knew that trade does more than diplomacy and armies to bring peoples together.*

*Alexander's greatness came from his vision and his leadership by example.*

**Question.** What lessons can we learn from Alexander's example, and how would they apply to Profit?

## LESSONS

What can we learn from Alexander's leadership?

- Right from his childhood, Alexander proved that he was both observant and a measured risk taker. All the adults around him saw the stallion's wild behavior and immediately judged it as impossible to train. On the surface, that would have seemed to be a valid assumption. Alexander looked at the horses' behavior and wondered why it was behaving that way. As a result, he saw that the animal was startled by its own shadow. Nevertheless, trying to ride a frightened horse was risky but, since Alexander saw the stallion begin to calm down, he figured that all that energy could be put to good use, and ran the risk by hopping on its back and riding away.

- Alexander led by example and from the front line. Contact with reality comes from the front line; in business the front line is where the customers are.
- He thought big and took on huge challenges, but he had prepared for them and also monitored them closely.
- He had absolute confidence in his own ability, and shared that feeling with his men, which gave them confidence in themselves.
- He looked where others did not, and saw what they couldn't. This talent became invaluable when he and his army entered into combat.
- He was daring and unconventional, which often scared his generals, but he was successful and that spoke for itself.
- He was realistic. Not only did he meet huge challenges, but he knew what it took to motivate his men to fight. (Of course, like at the battle of Issus, if your back is against a river, you have no choice but to fight as hard as you can.)
- He set clear goals and established equally clear rules for achieving them.
- He welcomed diversity and insisted his men do likewise.
- He took full responsibility when things went wrong and did all he could to make up for it.
- He helped his men overcome fears generated by uncertainty: Any new challenge will involve uncertainty about the end result. He made it clear that the fault, if there was one, would lie with him and not the people who reported to him.
- He carefully and constantly negotiated his way with both internal and external key players.
- He challenged his men to free themselves from self-imposed

limitations and opened their eyes to their real potential if they dare take on more daring goals.

- Was Alexander a perfect leader? No, no one ever is, but what he did wrong hurt himself more than his men.

## HOW DO TODAY'S LEADERS HANDLE TOUGH CHALLENGES AND SITUATIONS?

When the economy hits a recession, their immediate reaction is to cut back, and discount prices. What are the pluses and the minuses of these decisions? What are the assumptions behind them?

On cutting back, the assumptions are that there is too much of some things, and that cutting back will have an immediate effect on reducing costs. Depending on what you are cutting back, some costs and expenses can delay quite a while before the reduction can be felt.

In their hurry to cut back, companies often cut the wrong things that have a negative effect on production, customer service, and employee morale. Conclusion: Assumptions can be dangerous, and quick fixes are often both wrong and useless.

With regard to discounting because the competition is doing it, cutting prices does not guarantee increased or retained sales. It assumes that price is the only thing that customers care about; some do, but many don't. It also assumes that lowering prices is the only option for retaining customers. It is not.

There are many other things that can retain customers such as superb customer service. During the 2008, 2009 recession many insurance companies offered amazingly low prices that probably attracted lots of customers, but later lost them because of inferior service when the clients had valid claims.

**Conclusion:** Doing what everybody else is doing without exploring other options first can be costly and useless.

*Question. What can we learn from Alexander's example of submitting himself to the same hardships as his troops?*

Alexander led his soldiers through many extremely tough times in dangerous situations and battles, yet they stuck by him. He led by example and his men respected him for it. In tough economic times, many high-level executives continue to overspend on themselves while demanding that their employees do more with less. It doesn't work.

**Conclusion:** People will follow leaders whom they respect if those leaders have shown respect and consideration for the employees.

*Question. What can we learn from Alexander's approach to solving the Gordian Knot?*

The priests tried to fool Alexander into trying to solve what was probably an unsolvable problem and a hoax to begin with. Instead, he literally cut to the bottom line by ignoring the parameters offered by the priests and finding his own solution. In business, we are often asked to solve problems that are defined and framed by others, but quite often their definitions are wrong, and probably based on faulty assumptions.

**Conclusion:** Do not accept other people's definitions of Profit problems without first analyzing them yourself.

*Question. What can we learn from Alexander's decision to take on the most powerful ruler and his armies?*

What most people don't know about that decision is that Alexander had recently inherited his army from his father who had been assassinated shortly before. How would you feel if you suddenly became the top decision maker of a powerful organization with 35,000 employees to pay and feed?

His father had just conquered Greece, and there were no more enemies to fight. Alexander could have disbanded the army and just lived a very comfortable life within the kingdom he had inherited. Instead, Alexander put that army to good use by conquering new lands. That was the equivalent of assuming the leadership of the leading company in the United States market, and deciding to take on the global market.

**Conclusion:** You can't shrink your way to growth. It is smarter to think bigger and take on larger challenges.

## ONE MORE EXAMPLE OF THE POWER OF INNOVATIVE LEADERSHIP

One more thing that substantially influenced Alexander's success was his father's military innovations. Phillip's Macedonian army was famous for its Phalanxes, troops gathered in a solid square of 100 or more that advanced relentlessly against their enemies. An innovation introduced was the 18 footlong spears or lances that the troops used to reach the enemy at a distance that made their swords and shorter spears almost useless.

Another innovation was the catapult, basically a larger version of the crossbow that, like the 18 foot spears, allowed the Macedonians to injure and kill enemy soldiers at a distance.

And yet another innovation was the siege tower, which made it possible for the Macedonians to attack enemy walled cities, which Alexander used to conquer the city of Tyre in the Middle East.

A true leader is one that uses innovative change as a competitive advantage.

**Note.** Alexander the Great's Greatest Weakness: EGO! Watch out for it.

*Question. What innovations are you working on currently that will beat the competition at a distance?*

## SUMMARY

You can accomplish anything in life, provided that you do not mind who gets the credit. Harry S. Truman

There are many different types of leadership. In the Business Leader Ship, however, *the best leaders are those who bring out the best in others.* If you want to grow and profit, you need to engage the crew that will make that goal possible. How you choose to do that is your business, but if you do it wrong you will lose the ship and the business. On the other hand, if you follow the insights provided here, you will have a good ship, and a business that grows and increases profits along the way.

**Note.** A survey of managers throughout the United States revealed that on an average most of them devoted only 15 percent of their time to managing. The survey did not indicate why only 15 percent.

Some questions you may want to consider:

- Why do you think those managers do not devote more time to managing?
- Is it because they are so efficient that they don't need more?
- Could it be that they are so busy with their jobs that they just don't have time for more?
- Is it because they do not like to manage?
- Maybe they don't see any benefit from paying more attention to their subordinates?
- Does it have to do with the way their jobs are designed?
- Do they have too many people reporting to them?
- Could it be that they do not see their role as leaders?
- Perhaps they do not have enough staff and find themselves doing work that others should do?
- Maybe they just don't know enough about managing and leadership?
- Could it be that they don't feel they have a good staff?
- Or, is it simply because they feel they should be spending their time on what they know best and where they have expertise?
- Take a look at some of the managers in your organization and try to determine how much time they spend on managing and how well (or poorly) they do it. What might be the right amount of time to dedicate to managing?

# CHAPTER ELEVEN
# Preparing for Tomorrow's Profit and Growth Challenges

---

*"If we all did things we are capable of doing,*
*we would literally astound ourselves."*
Thomas Edison

---

## WHERE HAVE YOU BEEN, ARE NOW, AND GOING? LIFE IS ABOUT PATTERNS

As mentioned earlier, Peter Drucker said, "The best way to plan the future is to create it." That is true, but in business, if you want to create the right future, you must first develop a sense of how people and the world they live in are changing.

To do that, learn to look for patterns. From our earliest childhood we learn to look for patterns. The newborn baby cries, and it gets fed. After that, it has only to cry to get fed. A pattern is established and memorized. After a number of years, however, most patterns become commonplace; eventually they become subconscious and we don't pay much attention to them anymore.

We don't normally look for patterns in the commonplace. That's why we think it is commonplace. As a result, we miss seeing how the world around us is changing. *Most change is a subtle process,* **interrupted occasionally by violent events.** Pilots, for example, define flying as "hours of monotony interrupted by brief moments of intense panic."

Farmers say that in July you can actually hear the corn growing. I don't how true that is but it wouldn't surprise me. It could be the summer breeze gently rustling the stalks, but you'd have to sit in the middle of a cornfield in the hot summer and observe and listen very carefully if you wanted to detect the subtle patterns of growth.

We live in such a fast-paced, multi-tasking world today that we don't have time to notice what's happening around us - unless it shocks our senses. The days go by so fast that even summer is usually over before we finally got around to enjoying it.

## In the Business World

The same thing happens in the business world. To prepare for the future, we must take a good look at the present. In this chapter, we are going to explore the changing business environment in general and of companies. Instead of offering answers (like the newscasters and politicians), we will simply ask the kinds of questions that uncover hidden patterns and will hopefully lead us to useful answers.

Why would you want to do this? It sounds like a lot of work. Well, maybe it is and maybe it isn't. But even if it were, there are good reasons why you should go ahead with the questioning process. You need to think for yourself about those things that others will not think through for you. No one out there can tell you what to do about change in your own business because only you know the history of your company. Don't let others think for you! Don't accept their assumptions. You've got to do it yourself.

And when you do, you will begin to see the unseen changes that have been affecting your business. You will understand how things came to be as they are, and why they must be changed. And, most important, you will have the elements you need to make the decisions that will guide not only your company's future but also your own.

## QUESTIONS

There are many questions we could and should ask about the future of our business, in fact too many. For the sake of time I have reduced them to three questions with several subsets each. As you will see, they raise more questions than answers.

The three major questions we should be asking about our business are:

1. Is my company's business design right for the times?
2. Are we offering what customers will want?
3. Do we have the right leadership for the times?

Let's take a look at them, and as we go along, you'll notice that each question and sub-question can lead to many more questions:

### IS MY COMPANY'S BUSINESS DESIGN RIGHT FOR THE TIMES?

Most companies have been around for a long time. If we were to compare them to people who have been around for a long time, we might think of our grandparents or great-grandparents. A business design is the structure that the company has developed to serve its customers.

What would you think of a Great-Great Grandmother whose best years were in the Roaring 20's and who still dresses like a flapper? Well, there are many companies that do the equivalent. They are still operating as if the world hadn't changed since the company's foundation. Their structure was designed for a different time, market, and customer. Is it any wonder that they're having problems trying to cope with the changing times? Think of Sears, the now defunct Montgomery Ward, Woolworth's, the major airlines, and many struggling companies. They're stuck in time. Is your company stuck in time? All companies are to some degree, and to the degree that they are **so are their problems coping with change.**

How do we find out if our company's business design is obsolete? To do this we must keep in mind the following two points:

- You can't understand the present if you don't study the past.
- You can't prepare for the future if you don't understand the present.

Let's start with the past.
When was the company founded?

- What was the world like at that time?
- How has it changed?
- How has the company changed?

In most cases, the world has changed more than the company, but many of the companies' decisions that still stand today were made back then.
What market did it target?

- What was the market like at that time?
- Who were the competitors?
- Are we still addressing that market?

Markets and competitors are changing all the time, but are we changing to the same extent? And if we haven't what should we be changing?
What was the customer profile?

- Are we still selling to the same kinds of people?
- How have the demographics changed?
- Has the geographic profile changed?

We live in a world with a population that is approaching 7 billion, and 95 percent of them live outside the United States. The population of the United States is over 325 million and rapidly becoming far more diverse. The likelihood is that no matter where you are operating, you are no longer dealing with the same customer profile.

What channels were used to get the product to the customer?

- Why were those channels chosen?
- How have they changed?
- Are there new channels we should explore?

The original channels chosen by the company may have been focused on close-by regions. Cities, towns, and suburbs have grown and expanded widely. People are busier and it is harder for them to find the time to personally visit stores. Channels used to involve retail, wholesale, direct buying, direct mail, catalogs, media ads, and door-to-door sales. Nowadays, add drive-by, telemarketing, Internet, FedEx, plus overseas sources.

That was then. This is now. What about tomorrow?

- Was the design right for the times?
- Is it now?
- Were we in the right markets?
- Are we now?
- Were those the right customers to target?
- Are they now?
- Were those the right channels?
- Are they now?
- What about tomorrow?

The design may have been right for the times when the company was established, and so was your car, but – is it now? New markets and market segments are appearing every day all around the world. As populations age, people immigrate to other countries, middle classes grow, and older, traditional markets begin to fade away. Take a hard look at your customers: where are the new ones coming from and what are they like? What percentage of your customers has been with you for more than 5 years?

How must our company change?

The answer to this question is contained in the answers to the above questions. List them on a separate page and look for patterns. Is there a recurrent theme that seems to run through all the answers?

Are we offering what customers will want?

As your customers' priorities change, so must your business designs. For example, Montgomery Ward was structured to serve the customers of the 1940's and stayed that way into the 1990s when changing times caught up with it.

Have our customers changed?

- Are we serving the same customer base?
- Do they still live in the same areas?
- Are they the same generations?

The Hippies are gone (for the most part), the Boomers are retiring, people are moving into the suburbs and, in some places, they are moving back into the cities.

How have they changed?

- Is the family unit the same?
- Do they live differently?
- Are their needs different?

The percentage of single mothers has grown, education is taking more years, people are waiting much longer to get married, gay market is increasing, fewer families have dinner together, mobile phones have made people and businesses far more mobile, and many old jobs are vanishing while new ones are becoming a larger percentage of the total. Covid-19 has dramatically changed how and where people work. All of these changes imply that more people are living differently and have different needs.

How have their preferences changed?

- Do they dress the same?
- Do they have the same driving needs?
- Do they still enjoy the same type of entertainment?

Casual is the predominant business attire, places are increasingly farther away while the price of gasoline fluctuates, and the variety of entertainment sources and options is broader than ever.

What trends affect our offerings?

- Have our customers' perception of time changed?
- Has convenience become more important?
- Have discount stores impacted their buying habits?

Time is increasingly scarce and more valuable, people feel more pressured, and as a result convenience has become of greater importance. People are willing to pay more to save time and avoid inconvenience. Discount stores have continued to grow in number and variety.

How must our offerings change?

- Should our products be replaced by new ones?

- Should we continue to stress product features?
- Should we offer only what we manufacture?

If not replaced, products and services should at least be modified and updated. Benefits must be stressed more than features. Where is it written that you must manufacture everything you sell? On the contrary, it might be wiser to increase the amounts of products obtained from other sources.

Do we have the right leadership for the times?

- What were the criteria for leadership in the past?
- Was management more important than leadership?
- Was selection restricted to males only?
- Were academic credentials a leading factor?

The criteria for leadership has changed notably. Bossy command and order types no longer fit the needs of new times and generations. In the past, management was more about supervising rather than directing and leading. Selection has been broadened to bring in more women and minorities. Academic credentials were less important than today, but now they are a basic requirement although not the most critical element of leadership. Often vocational or focused Associates Degrees are needed now.

What are today's requirements?

- How do today's needs impact leadership?
- What do we expect of today's leaders?
- How important is vision in leadership?

Today's gender, generation, and diversity demand higher emotional IQ on the part of leaders. Today, leaders are not only expected to require accountability but also to develop their followers.

What will they be tomorrow?

- Will tomorrow's pressures be greater or lesser than today's?
- What will be different in tomorrow's business environment?
- Will tomorrow's leaders come from the same backgrounds as today's?

Growing global competition is already generating greater performance pressure. Expect it to increase continually, although evolving communication does help expedite processes. Tomorrow's business environment will provide greater, faster, and more diversified communication, but expectations will also grow as companies work at expanding globally. Unexpected change will come quicker and require increasingly rapid response. Tomorrow's leaders will come from more than the traditional financial, production, and marketing backgrounds. Entrepreneurial skills will be in growing demand everywhere.

How must our criteria change?

- Where will we look for leaders tomorrow?
- What will we ask of them?
- How will we reward them?

The real business world can be very confusing, but Max De Pree former CEO of Herman Mille Furniture, hit the nail on the head when he said, "It is the job of every leader to describe reality." Do you offer a realistic perspective balanced with a positive can- do attitude?

We want our leaders to be big thinking visionaries with an ability to see beyond the immediate, to be creative and innovative problem solvers who are bottom line and customer focused. We will ask them to grow the company, themselves, and their people while increasing Profit and customer satisfaction. Rewarding will be both financial and recognition along with offering them ever more exciting challenges and opportunities.

**In the future, everyone will have to be a leader.**
**So, who's in charge of the future?**
**YOU ARE!**

## SUMMARY

We started out with three questions and we ended up with far more, *and we're only beginning.* I'm sure that as you followed the questioning sequence, you thought of more questions that could be asked. The process is practically endless, but it is one of the most effective management tools you will ever use.

They say that the person who asks the questions controls the conversation. I would add that the person who asks the questions not only gets the most answers, but also becomes a more effective leader and manager. Of equal importance will be the ability to probe unquestioned answers.

From my own background in the corporate world, and also from my consulting experience, I can tell you that the higher you rise in the management hierarchy, the better you will have to be at asking questions. Why, because the higher you rise the more distant you are from the front line of operations and the revenue generating customer. The people at the top of all companies tend to become professional question-askers. You could say that necessity has driven them to become professional interrogators.

It is the job of these question-askers to challenge every aspect of the business and to develop an inspiring vision of a better future that will guide and motivate the whole company team to rise to greater levels. It is also your job. It is the job of everyone in business.

As a consultant, I have a strategy that I try to stick to. It is to always question the client's definition of his problem. Experience has taught me that clients don't always identify the right problem. As I mentioned earlier, there is no right solution to the wrong problem. If the client had defined his problem properly, he would have solved it already - and my services would not be needed. That's another reason why questions are so important; they help find the truth, or at least get closer to it.

**To find the truth and generate the future prosperity of your company, you must ask good, probing questions.** Your chances of finding something improve substantially when you actually and actively looking for it.

Shakespeare had it right when he had Hamlet aske the ultimate question: **"To be or not to be. That is the question."**

**The answer to the questions we have asked here will determine whether your company is to be - or not to be.**

## THE POWER OF PROFIT AND BEYOND

*What would a world without profit look like?*

We discussed this at the beginning of the Introduction; that was about the power of profit so far, now let's take a look at the beyond part.

Imagine a world that is improved every time you contribute to generating and increasing profit and allow yourself to feel good about it. Know that you are working for a good purpose.

The above statements may seem naïve to some, but they are not. We all know that there are greedy and dishonest persons out there trying to make a profit through dishonest schemes and scams, but thanks to you and people like you, they are a minority and will remain one.

## JOBS NOT COMING BACK

Question: Why hasn't the stimulus brought more jobs back?

Answer: Because many of them are gone forever. The economic and business models that created them in the first place are no longer there. This is part of an ongoing economic evolution. At the beginning of the 20th" century, almost half of the U.S. population lived on farms producing food for themselves and the rest of the nation. By the end of the century, thanks to technology which allowed farms to produce much more with much less, and to urban growth, less than 3 percent of the population grew more than enough food to supply not only the entire population (now three times greater than in 1900) but also to sell billions of dollars' worth to the rest of the world.

In manufacturing, over the last 50 years we have been seeing something similar due to automation, robotics, computerization, lean manufacturing, outsourcing, and improved logistics and techniques; we now produce far more with much less. Further, the purpose of a company is not to operate plants, or even to create jobs, but to create value and customer delight while generating a worthwhile return on shareholder investment.

Back in the early nineties we began to see the same thing happening in the service and administration areas, as a result of computerization, outsourcing, automation, and the fast-growing application of artificial intelligence. It was evident then that the vanishing jobs were no longer necessary and would not be coming back. As happened during the agricultural and manufacturing evolutions, the people who lost those jobs would have to either find different types of jobs or create other ways of making a living.

The population of the United States is, and will continue to be, growing, but the creation of jobs may not keep up with that pace. Old companies will be disappearing, and new ones will appear, but that does not mean an equal number of jobs will be around. Obviously, current generations will eventually retire (if that is still an option in the future), and many but not all of those jobs will be filled by newer generations.

Stimulus, making money more accessible to business, may help some companies to survive, and others to even grow, but it is not the business of companies to create jobs. If anything, it might even be desirable for them to operate without employees. Plants are becoming so automated that there is talk about them operating "in the dark", that is, without employees.

So, how are future generations going to make a living? The current extension of unemployment benefits cannot go on forever ~ or can it? Is it the government's job to feed the people? No, but if it doesn't, will the people allow it to remain in power?

At the time of the Roman Empire, over a period of 700 years since its founding, the city of Rome grew from a small village to a population of a million. Farmlands shifted from small family operations to become huge landowner estates. After losing their farms, many people moved to the city of Rome, thus its tremendous population growth. But, unlike the United States, there were no new machines to work the land, and food production declined to the point where the government had to import food, mostly from Egypt, to feed the population. Of course, politicians took advantage of this economic disadvantage to increase their power and wealth.

Will we follow this path? I don't think so, but we do need to tackle the job elimination trend and create alternate ways of earning a living. There are parts of the United States where there are not many jobs simply because there are no factories or large corporate headquarters in the area. How do people make a living? Some of them own farms, others provide essential services such as police, fire protection, healthcare, sanitation, and so on. Others, open stores that supply the multiple needs of local residents and, where seasonal tourism is part of the economy, provide related services. Many earn their living by holding a series of seasonal part-time jobs. Will this be our future? Maybe not, but it could provide a part of it. The growth of online businesses and services will probably continue almost endlessly in the years ahead. Could alternative energy sources provide new industries? What new service industries will be needed?

What is clear is that just supplying credit and money to industry will not bring back all the jobs that are destined to disappear due to obsolescence and technological advances. The one thing we must do is to prepare today's emerging generations to meet the challenges of dramatic change that lie ahead.

More than ever before, adaptability to change will be essential. We must use our ability to find creative solutions, something that has enabled us to survive millions of years of threats, disasters, and challenging "un-expecteds".

Looking beyond today, where will profits come from in the future? More important, where will

Your profits come from?

Possibilities lie in the prevailing technological influences that we have:

- Automation
- Artificial intelligence
- Nanotechnology
- Stem cell research
- Biotechnology
- Genetics
- Quantum physics
- Superconductors
- Supercomputers
- Robotics
- Advanced telecommunications
- E-commerce
- Alternative energy

Each of the above can become either a technology you will use, or a growing market segment you can sell to, or both. Either way, they can become sources of profits, that is, if you look at them with those possibilities in mind.

*In the end, however, your profits will come from and be produced by people, and that is where you will need to focus your attention now and the future. As people change, so will their preferences and needs, and so will your markets.*

What are some of the characteristics of the generation of future consumers and leaders? Here is some information from a recent survey:

- More than 40 percent of young people doubt they can achieve their goals
- 70 percent wish they had more opportunities to help them fulfill their dreams
- Fewer than 60 percent feel a sense of purpose
- Less than 65 percent are motivated to achieve
- Fewer than 30 percent feel they have skills like planning and decision-making
- 25 percent of all public high school students fail to graduate on time, if at all.
- 50 percent of African-Americans and Hispanics fail to graduate on time, if at all.
- 75 percent of those incarcerated did not graduate from high school.

The good news is what these statistics do not tell you is that they represent yesterday's trends, not necessarily tomorrow's. More and more minorities are graduating from high school and going on to college. There are more women in colleges than men. 85 percent of adolescents who get training in success skills graduate on time, resulting in a 50 percent drop in welfare dependency.

It is estimated that by the year 2050, almost 50 percent of the U.S. population will be composed of people who we now call minorities. What that statistic does not tell you is that, although currently considered minorities, by then they will no longer be or be viewed as such, and they will be better educated and much more technologically savvy than today's generations. Not only that, but they will also be more flexible thinkers and definitely more creative.

Our society will be more diverse and more integrated than ever before, a fact that will provide our nation with a competitive advantage because the rest of the nations around the world are just now starting to deal with and integrate minorities.

You have the power to develop solutions to not only today's job crisis but also tomorrow's. Just as technology eliminated so many jobs, it can create more businesses and jobs that will provide for future generations. Thanks to technology and automation, and other technologies, more new businesses of kinds never seen before (who would have predicted a business called Google?) will open the doors to many new kinds of businesses of all different sizes. Many of these businesses will be the source of income for new entrepreneurs and generate millions of new jobs for today's and tomorrow's unemployed. By generating new profits and increasing existing ones, you will be contributing to the welfare of the world and will make it a better place for all.

Bottom line: people will continue to be the source of profit, but they won't be the same as today's people neither as employees or consumers. Therefore, to be profitable, businesses will have to change in order to keep up with changes in the sources of Profit.

The principles presented in this book will help you contribute to that goal. Go for it! Keep going! And come back to this book on a regular basis for reinforcement of both your skills and your motivation!

# Epilogue

As you continue to pursue Sustainable Profit Growth for your organization, company, or business, you will run into an almost never-ending list of problems. It can be stressful and, at times, even down-right discouraging.

Do not give up! You are much better than you ever thought. Just think of all the problems you faced and solved in the past and did it when you had even less experience than now.

This book is designed to help you diagnose and solve many of the problems that await you, but no book can answer them all. For that reason, I have included my contact information below. Feel free to contact me at any time. I would love to hear from you. Between us, we should be able to come up with some good solutions.

To give you a somewhat different perspective of problems, I would like to share a story. Years ago, a friend of mine told me about something that happened on his return from a business trip to California. On the return flight, he sat next to an elderly woman. She turned out to be Dr. Lillian Gilbreth.

Do you recognize the name? Lillian Gilbreth was the wife of Frank Gilbreth. They were famous efficiency experts at the beginning of the 20th century. Still don't recognize the name? They are the couple that had 12 children and about whom the book, "Cheaper By The Dozen", was written and later converted into at least two very popular movies.

Mr. Gilbreth died at a rather early age and left his wife with 12 children to raise and educate. Not only did she raise all of them, but also got them all through college and onto professional careers. As if that were not enough, she went on to get a PhD in engineering and built her own consulting business. She served as advisor to **Presidents Hoover, Roosevelt, Eisenhower, Kennedy and Johnson** on civil defense, war production and rehabilitation of the physically handicapped. Dr. Gilbreth was returning on that late flight from a consulting engagement in California. By now, she was in her eighties.

Amazed at her energy and endurance, my friend asked her if she didn't find managing problems rather stressful at her age. Dr. Gilbreth smiled and said, "Every day I thank God for problems. They keep me alive and active. What would life be like without problems?"

That is my question to you: What would life be like without problems?

Yes, they can wear you down, but they are the source of discovery, innovation, and accomplishment. So, when things get tough, think of that amazing woman, Dr. Lillian Gilbreth, and give thanks for your challenges, your problems, and the talent you were given to solve them.

**Problems are the source of profits. A world without problems would be a world without profits. Now, get out there, tackle those problems, and make your PROFIT!**

Best wishes,

*Mike Wynne*
Global President
International Management Consulting Associates
mykwyn@aol.com
www.imcaonline.com

# Appendix

The Tip Sheets and Checklist that appear in the following pages are extracted primarily from the main body of the book. There are many ways you can use them to manage your staff and teams. For example, as:

- Reminder Lists
- Checklists
- Delegation Aids
- Operation Lists
- Training Aids
- Project Aids
- Planning Aids
- Monitoring Aids
- Control Lists
- Goal Setting Guides

You can even copy and bind them into workbooks for all the above.

# Tip Sheet: Smart Business Practices

- Reduce staff by attrition
- Strengthen your team
- Improve your product mix
- Upgrade your customer service
- Measure employee performance
- Recognize good performance
- Set up a performance improvement system
- Weed out poor performers
- Train constantly
- Analyze your processes
- Re-design your customer policies
- Develop and launch new products
- Review and analyze your business model
- Set goals for reducing variable costs
- Set goals for reducing fixed costs
- Analyze and reduce finished product inventories
- Analyze and reduce supplies inventories
- Broaden your product lines with purchased products
- Leverage all assets to the max
- Get rid of unproductive assets
- Form purchasing cooperatives

# Tip Sheet: The Smart Businesses Four Basic Growth Strategies

## EXISTING CUSTOMERS

Selling More Existing Products and Services to Existing Customers

- Increase share of existing customers
- Offer volume incentives to existing clients
- Offer prompt payment incentives to same clients
- Increase order/unit size
- Deliver faster
- Reposition existing product concept
- Combine with other products/services
- Create subcategories of existing products/services
- Offer discounts to existing customers
- Lower price
- Add value
- Develop new uses for existing products/services
- Rename existing products.
- Train clients in better and additional usage
- Offer credit incentives to existing customers
- Increase advertising
- Increase promotion
- Tele-market to existing clients
- Track usage and offer reminders
- Manage client's inventory
- Produce/assemble product at customer site
- Increase number and frequency of sales calls
- Help clients sell what they buy from you
- Offer advertising and promotion co-ops.
- Change packaging

Selling New Products to Existing Customers

- Develop modified versions of specific products and services for other uses
- Offer technology upgrades
- Create new packaging sizes
- Bundle products/services
- Un-bundle others
- Develop products/services for new price levels
- Piggyback products made by others with yours
- Increase information content of existing products - make "smart"
- Add-on to existing products creating new categories
- Create new brands
- Customize existing products to existing customers
- Offer same customized version for other existing customers
- Consider "downstream" products/services
- Ask customers what improvements they would like
- Offer customers the capability to make their own version of your product
- Create special occasion, one-time-only event, versions of products
- Develop successor, "son-of, products
- Develop products that perform several functions - Swiss Army Knife approach
- Increase number of features of existing products
- Develop new products and new uses to go with them.

## NEW CUSTOMERS

Selling Existing Products and Services to New Customers

- Increase number of prospects
- Offer volume incentives to prospects

- Offer prompt payment incentives to new clients
- Increase order/unit size
- Deliver faster
- Reposition existing product concept
- Combine with other products/services
- Create subcategories of existing products/services
- Offer discounts to existing customers
- Lower price
- Add value
- Develop new uses for existing products/services
- Rename existing products.
- Train clients in better and additional usage
- Offer credit incentives to existing customers
- Increase advertising
- Increase promotion
- Tele-market to existing clients
- Track usage and offer reminders
- Manage client's inventory
- Produce/assemble product at customer site
- Increase number and frequency of sales calls
- Help clients sell what they buy from you
- Offer advertising and promotion co-ops.
- Change packaging

Selling New Products to New Customers

- Develop modified versions of specific products/services for other uses
- Offer technology upgrades
- Create new packaging sizes
- Bundle products/services
- Un-bundle others
- Develop products/services for new price levels
- Piggyback products made by others with yours

- Increase information content of existing products
- Add special new products for new groups of customers
- Create new brands
- Customize existing products to new customers
- Consider "downstream" products/services
- Ask new customers what improvements they would like
- Offer customers the capability to make their own version of your product
- Create special occasion, one-time-only event, versions of products
- Develop successor, "son-of" products
- Develop products that perform several functions - Swiss Army Knife approach
- Increase number of features of existing products
- Develop new uses for new and existing products

# Sustainable Profit Checklist

*Brewing Profit Storm Ahead?*

*Time to batten down the performance hatches, seal any profit leaks, set a new strategic course, and steer your company with great executive care and skill.*

We hope this free checklist of 42 key indicators of a brewing Profit storm in a business will help you prevent a perfect storm in your company. Take a look at the indicators. If more than any five apply to your company, a Profit storm may be headed your way.

| Marketing Related | Management Related |
|---|---|
| Falling sales | Product driven management |
| Shrinking markets | Weak managerial skills |
| Customer inertia | No upgrades |
| Low or negative profit | Insufficient buying options |
| Losing customers | Inadequate pricing revenues |
| Competition with better products | Organizational silos |
| Competition with new products | Unleveraged suppliers |
| Price competition | Negative attitudes |
| Unprofitable customers | Rising costs |
| Poor product mix | Poor negotiating skills |
| No upgrades | Misguided priorities |
| Changing markets | Lack of resources |
| Selling on price | Rising expenses |
| Low customer service | Inadequate cash flow |
| Price competition | Excess inventories |
| Customer preferences changing | Misallocation of resources |
| Customer turnover | Low productivity |
| Unexciting offerings | Lacking process analysis |
| Lackluster products | Unhappy employees |

| Marketing Related | Management Related |
|---|---|
| Undifferentiated products | Unleveraged assets |
| Low comparative value products | Yesterday's Technology |
| Traditional solutions no longer work | Too many discounts |

These are the symptoms. Now, it is up to you to define the problem and develop the right solution. Confused? Just go back to the book and you will find your right solution!

# Tip Sheet: Key Profit Thoughts to Keep in Mind.

Because People are your best source of Profits

- Excellence starts with people; they are the key to Profit!
- If you want to be more profitable, look to your people first.
- Hiring the best and setting them free beats micromanaging. (Question. Does setting them free, make you somewhat uneasy? Are your people ready to be set free? Should they be?)
- Highly motivated and well rewarded people who are free to do their own thinking, rather than just being told what to do, produce more profits and fewer problems.
- No company is ever stronger than its people, and its people-strength is the product of talent, motivation, training and the way they are treated.
- Creating a motivating vision and getting buy-in, leverages the power of purpose.
- Finally, customers are people, and profits are the best sign of their satisfaction with the values you provide through your products and services.

Regarding Strategy and Structure

- Developing company-wide understanding of the Mechanics of Profit increases attention to productivity. *When people believe in something, they do something about it.*
- Planning and implementing ambitious, reality-grounded growth strategies increases day-to- day focus
- Developing profitable pricing strategies generates higher revenues.
- Designing profitable product mixes leads to greater revenues and gross profits.

- Awareness of the need to leverage resources creates new sources of revenues

Why building Exceptional Teams is essential to Growth and Profit

- Building and unleashing exceptional teams ensures progress.
- Exceptional teams grow productivity faster and consistently. It *takes a team to win!*
- It takes team effort to control costs and expenses

Innovation is the key to Thriving and Surviving

- The best way to look for innovative solutions is to look for problems.
- Innovation that creates true customer value increases marketing success.
- Today's customers constantly demand new products and services.

# Show Me the Money Checklist

What kinds of numbers should you be collecting and analyzing? Financials come to mind first.

Business is about money, so you need numbers that can answer questions such as:

- Where is it coming from?
- Where is it going?
- What costs too much?
- What requires more money?
- Where are you not earning enough?
- Where are you spending too much?

Then there are the numbers associated with Production:

- How much is being produced?
- Is it enough, or too little?
- Is it too costly, or not enough?
- Is it being dedicated to the right efforts?
- Is the return on money invested in production good enough, or is it generating losses?
- Are employees being productive enough?
- Is production being generated fast enough?
- Are inventories too high or too low?
- Is space being used properly?
- Is quality as high as it should be?
- Are designs helping or hindering production?
- What is the profitability of the various pieces of equipment?

Numbers are essential to managing Sales and Marketing:

- Are prices right?
- What about sales volume?

- How is the product mix performing both in terms of units sold and profit per line and per unit?
- Which territories are doing well, and why?
- Which are not, and why?
- Re: salespeople: which are meeting expectations and which are not? Which salespeople are profitable, and which are not?
- Which customers are growing in purchases of our products and services?
- Which are shrinking?
- Which customers are profitable and which are not?
- Which customers are demanding too much time, money and effort?
- Are we spending enough or too much on promotions and advertising?
- Are we building a solid Sales and Marketing base for growth?

Numbers are extremely important in managing human resources.

- Do we have too many or too few employees?
- Are we paying them too high or too low?
- Are we measuring their performance properly?
- Are they costing us too much?
- Are our benefit plans appropriate for the purposes of our company's future?
- Are we tracking employee productivity?
- Are our Accounts Receivable up to date?
- Are we generating enough cash to cover our Accounts Payable and Payroll?
- Do we have enough cash in the bank?
- Have we established a solid relationship with the banks with which we work?
- Are we planning far enough ahead of our needs?
- Are our liabilities growing faster than our assets?

- Are we getting the most out of our investments and assets?

As you can see from the above, there are many things that require tracking, analyzing, planning, and budgeting. It is vital that you devote the necessary time to absorbing and analyzing the numbers of all aspects of your business.

# Strategic Thinking Checklist

Strategic thinking is vital to your success and to that of your people. You and your team will save a lot of time, effort, and money by thinking along these lines. It is about distinguishing:

- The strategic from the tactical
- The vital from the trivial
- The important from the urgent
- The profitable from the unprofitable
- The short-term from the long-term
- The practical from the impractical
- The doable from the not doable
- The possible from the impossible
- The original from the copycat
- The probable from the improbable
- The necessary from the unnecessary.
- The reliable from the unreliable.
- What works from what does not work
- What must be done today instead of tomorrow
- Who has potential and who does not.
- Realities from just numbers
- Opportunities from problems.

**Comfort zones, routines and rituals are the enemies of strategic thinking. Questions are the lifeblood of strategic thinking.** *Never let a day go by without questioning something!*

# Tip Sheet: Profit Questions.

These are questions that you should ask yourself regarding your current gross profit situation:

- Where are your sales coming from? Why there?
- In terms of Gross Profit, which are the most profitable of the following?
  - g. Product lines
  - h. Products
  - i. Markets
  - j. Channels of distribution
  - k. Services
  - l. Clients
- Why are they more profitable?
- Who are your most successful competitors?
- Which of their products are most successful? Why?
- Which of your markets are changing? How and why?
- How is your customer base changing? Why?
- What innovations have you introduced in the last two years? Why?
- Which part of the Sustainable product or service cost is the biggest factor? Why? How do your product/service costs compare to those of your competitors; why?
- How do we measure efficiency? Why?
- How do your ratios compare with those of your industry? Why?
- How do you plan annual improvements in sales and costs? Why?
- How do you plan annual improvements in sales and production processes? Why?

# Pricing Strategy Checklist

Expect your prices to be challenged. Design your products and services to fully justify the prices you will charge. Different customers may have different values; identify those customers and the benefits they value, and design your products and services to delightfully satisfy their expectations. This way you will be defending your prices even before they are challenged.

- Do your products or services target high or low-price customers? Make it clear for the consumer, too.
- Does the image of your products or services lend itself to high price? The image you create for your products or services will determine their salability.
- The price you set for your products or services will also determine their image. Low prices rarely are associated with high level product image, just as high prices are usually associated with high level products.
- It is very hard to negotiate up from a price that is low. Better to create a new brand.
- It is easier to negotiate down from a high price but be sure it is clearly only a temporary action.
- Once you are identified with a low price, it is very hard to create an image of high-level products. Would buyers prefer a Lexus or a higher priced Toyota?
- Once you are identified with a high price, anything lower will damage your image, and a damaged image is almost impossible to retrieve.
- It is extremely unlikely that a single brand might successfully cover both low and high price products.
- The decision to compete as the perennially lowest price product or service is unsustainable because there are many competitors who will cut their price below yours, even if they lose money doing so.

- The decision to compete as the highest price product or service is equally unsustainable because sooner or later someone will either come up with a better, more attractive alternative, or one that is equally attractive at a lower price.
- Actually, you may be better off if you have low, medium, and higher-level products with prices that are in line with the differences between them. It is not the same as being positioned at either end of the market.
- If you are in a market of a temporary nature such as fads, shortages or current event related, you can have a Get-In-and-Get-Out strategy with a temporarily acceptable higher price, but with the knowledge that the demand or the price will eventually decrease, and you will exit the market then.
- If you are in at the beginning of a new market, you may be able to have higher prices simply because at this point there is not much competition, but there will be before long.
- As long as your product is perceived as providing high value, you will be able to charge a higher price. Value makes the buying decision easy.

## Tip Sheet: Charging for Value

- Are you giving away value? I hate to use airlines as an example, but remember when they provided meals for free?
- Are you providing services that you could charge for? Do you offer express delivery at no extra charge?
- What services could you create that would be chargeable? For example:
- Special delivery
- Repairs
- Exchanges
- Upgrades
- Extra products
- Parking space
- Valet parking
- Reduced waiting time
- Extended warranties
- Matching colors
- Designs
- Accessories
- Maintenance
- Information
- Reservations

Be careful with charging for things that previously were provided for free because it may cause customer resentment. How do you get around this? You do it by increasing the perceived value as a justification for a modest charge. However reluctantly, most of us are willing to pay for something that we perceive as new and improved, and therefore more valuable than what we used to get for free.

Sometimes, providing value for free is not necessarily a bad move, provided you are retrieving the cost of that value by continued profitable sales. Value adding is a strategy that helps you retain truly profitable customers, but don't waste it on customers who won't let you make a decent profit.

# Ways of Expressing Value Checklist

| | | | | |
|---|---|---|---|---|
| Speed | Energy | Productivity | Simplification | Relief |
| Earnings | Sales | Sales Growth | Gross Margin | Gross Profit |
| Safety | Security | Certainty | Loss Prevention | Learning |
| Cost savings | Excitement | Motivation | Worry Avoidance | Vitality |
| Aesthetics | Ease | Understanding | Change Facilitation | Cooperation |
| Innovation | Creativity | Quality | Operating Income | Continuity |
| Readiness | Convenience | Enjoyment | Skills Improvement | Comfort |
| Perception | Service | Reliability | Mistake Avoidance | Manpower |
| Efficiency | Information | Communication | Conflict Resolution | Anticipation |
| Satisfaction | Market Share | Share of Account | Competitive Edge | Turnover |
| Price Edge | Substitution | Disposal | Relationship | Inventory |
| Morale | Absenteeism | Productivity | Increased Value | Effort |

# Tip Sheet: 48 Smart Ways to Increase Your Sales

1. Increase share of existing customers
2. Offer volume incentives to existing clients Offer prompt payment incentives to same clients
3. Increase order/unit size
4. Deliver faster
5. Reposition existing product concept
6. Combine with other products/services
7. Create subcategories of existing products/services
8. Offer discounts to existing customers
9. Lower price
10. Add value
11. Develop new uses for existing products/services
12. Rename existing products.
13. Train clients in better and additional usage
14. Offer credit incentives to existing customers
15. Increase advertising
16. Increase promotion
17. Tele-market to existing clients
18. Track usage and offer reminders
19. Manage client's inventory
20. Produce/assemble product at customer site
21. Increase number and frequency of sales calls
22. Help clients sell what they buy from you
23. Offer advertising and promotion co-ops.
24. Change packaging
25. Develop modified versions of specific products/services for other uses
26. Offer technology upgrades
27. Create new packaging sizes
28. Bundle products/services
29. Un-bundle others
30. Develop products/services for new price levels

31. Piggyback products made by others with yours
32. Increase information content of existing products
33. Add-on to existing products creating new categories
34. Create new brands
35. Customize existing products to existing customers
36. Offer same customized version for other existing customers
37. Consider "downstream" products/services
38. Ask customers what improvements they would like
39. Offer customers the capability to make their own version of your product
40. Create special occasion, one-time-only event, versions of products
41. Develop successor, "son-of, products
42. Develop products that perform several functions - Swiss Army Knife approach
43. Increase number of features of existing products
44. Develop new products and new uses to go with them.
45. Offer products/services in new areas
46. Export
47. Find new users for existing products

# Customer Purchase Steps

When you think through the 11-step process that customers go through as they make an in-person purchase, ask yourself what could be done to make each step a better, more distinctive experience.

1. **Awareness.** The customer identifies a need.
2. **Education.** The customer searches for information that will improve his or her knowledge about the product and the offerings in the marketplace.
3. **Contact.** The customer telephones, e-mails, or visits retailers.
4. **Selection.** Customer selects certain piece or pieces of furniture at a specific retailer.
5. **Negotiation.** Customer and supplier seek mutually acceptable price and terms
6. **Acquisition.** The customer makes the buying decision.
7. **Delivery.** Furniture is delivered to the customer.
8. **Follow up.** Supplier checks customer satisfaction.
9. **Relationship.** Supplier stays in touch with customer.
10. **Repeat sale.** Customer returns to retailer for next purchase.
11. **Disposal.** Retailer helps customer dispose of old furniture.

# The 80/20 Reminder List

A minority of inputs generate the majority of output. Apply 80/20 analysis to all your company's activities. This pattern repeats itself in everything.

- 20% of clients generate 80% of sales
- 20% of products generate 80% of Gross Profit
- 20% of salespeople generate 80% of sales
- 20% of products generate 80% of inventory
- 20% of activities generate 80% of costs
- 20% of raw materials generate 80% of costs

# Cost Reduction Questions

- Are you using too much?
- Are you paying too much?
- Are you buying from only one source?
- Do you really need it?
- Can you replace it with something less expensive?
- Can you eliminate it?
- Can you import it cheaper?
- Can you combine or bundle it with other purchases at a lower price?
- Can you re-negotiate prices and terms? Are there better alternatives?
- Is shipping too expensive?
- Would it be less expensive if you bought it in larger quantities?
- Would it be less expensive if you bought it in larger quantities over a longer period?
- Can you get more help and services from the supplier?
- Can you pool resources with other buyers of the same products to get greater volume discounts?
- Can you get the supplier to stock it nearby?
- Can you outsource part of the operation to a supplier?
- Can you produce your own version?
- Should you buy out the supplier?
- Can you redesign or reformulate the product to be less expensive?
- Can you re-sell what you don't use?
- Can you negotiate better prices and terms?
- Are you using a better quality than needed?
- Is there a more efficient process that would use less of the product?
- Can you dilute it more?
- Can you produce it yourself?
- Is there a different version that might actually save money

because you would use much less?

- Can you get on-time delivery that would save money because you would not need as much inventory?

# Tip Sheet: Energy Cost Reduction Questions

Energy costs are becoming a growing cost factor and need careful attention. Currently, there are no inexpensive sources of energy, and one thing is for sure – there will not be any in the short run. Granted, wind is free and so is sunshine, but the cost of making them available is considerable. Coal is relatively cheaper than oil, but controlling its pollution impact is expensive. It pays to monitor energy costs closely, accumulate solid data, and look for better, less expensive alternatives.

- Do you analyze your energy costs on a regular basis?
- Have you designed an energy master plan for your business?
- Do you know where your energy is being used and how much?
- Do you have energy-saving policies and procedures?
- Are all the lights on in your building all night?
- Are you moving towards alternative energy sources?
- Do you have shades or blinds to keep out the hot summer sun?
- Have you checked windows and doors for leaks that admit cold air in the winter, or let cold air out during the summer?
- Are you recovering any of the energy being spent?
- How many pieces of equipment are left on all night?
- Do the temperature controls work properly? Or, does your place get so cold in the summer that employees have to open doors to let warm air in?
- Are there parts of the building where the circulation is inadequate and are too cold in the winter and too hot in the summer?
- Is the air in your plant clean?
- Is the lighting in your building adequate or does it cause eye strain?
- Are there enough electrical outlets for the growing amount

of electronic equipment required in today's business?

- Are you looking for ways to automate more tasks?
- Is anyone in your organization in charge of monitoring energy consumption?
- Have you considered switching your vehicles from fossil fuels to hybrids and other alternatives?
- Have you increased insulation as a way to lower both heating and air conditioning costs?
- Are you renegotiating energy contracts to obtain lower costs?
- Why not buy larger-than-you-need volumes of gasoline at lower prices, and share the excess with the employees offering them lower than gas station prices?
- Are you recycling water, and using it for non-drinking purposes?
- Are you collecting rainwater?
- Are you selling some waste products such as metals and paper to businesses that use them for their own production?

# Tip Sheet: Delivery Cost Reduction Questions

Getting the product to the customer can sometimes be a costly process. Questions you might ask:

- Can you outsource delivery and get even better results?
- Can you get customers to buy larger amounts so that you have fewer deliveries?
- Do you have the most efficient delivery vehicles?
- Do you have a standard rate for shipping, or one that varies according to the distance?
- Do you own your vehicles outright, or do you lease them?
- Are your vehicle maintenance costs too high?
- Can you program and plan your deliveries more efficiently to reduce number of trips and mileage?
- Is cargo space efficiently allocated for maximum loading?
- Is shipping dock properly designed for fastest loading and unloading?
- Are drivers properly trained to choose best delivery routes?
- Do vehicle insurance plans provide adequate coverage at good price?
- Should you consider increasing order size to reduce the number of unprofitable deliveries?
- Should you charge proportionately more for smaller order deliveries than larger ones?
- Are you charging enough for special deliveries?
- Do you allow or encourage customer pick up of their orders?
- Do you plan deliveries so drivers can pick up supplies on their return trips?
- Is your staff knowledgeable enough to handle international orders and deliveries?

# Tip Sheet: Manufacturing Cost Reduction Questions

Where are you...

- Spending the most?
- Investing the most?
- Using the most energy?
- Devoting the most labor?
- Consuming the most time?
- Causing the most problems?
- Generating the most rejects?
- Taking up the most space?
- Producing the least results?
- Finding it harder and more expensive to operate?

For example, in manufacturing what processes take the most time?

Sometimes, lengthy processes may actually represent only a minor part of the manufacturing; they might contribute little yet cost a lot. For example, in manufacturing where paint is applied to the product,

- How long does the drying in an oven take?
- What if the product requires several coats of different paints?
- How much is the Sustainable oven time?
- Does the product have to go around several times to pass through the same oven, or does it require several ovens which consume large amounts of energy and take up a large amount of space?

Some equipment takes longer to set up or maintain.

- If one line is used for manufacturing several products, does the equipment have to be re-set each time, and how long does that take?

- What is the cost of the downtime?

Other types of equipment may be very expensive, but aren't used that much.

- Is 80 percent of the equipment investment in equipment that is used only 20 percent of the time?
- Can this be outsourced?

What do you buy the most of? Whatever it is, that is where to look for expense reductions.

- Are you using too much?
- Are you paying too much?
- Are you buying from only one source?
- Do you really need it?
- Can you replace it with something less expensive?
- Can you eliminate it?
- Can you import it cheaper?
- Can you combine or bundle it with other purchases at a lower price?
- Can you re-negotiate prices and terms? Are there better alternatives?
- Is shipping too expensive?
- Would it be less expensive if you bought it in larger quantities?
- Would it be less expensive if you bought it in larger quantities over a longer period?
- Can you get more help and services from the supplier?
- Can you pool resources with other buyers of the same products to get greater volume discounts?
- Can you get the supplier to stock it nearby?
- Can you outsource part of the operation to a supplier?
- Can you produce your own version?
- Should you buy out the supplier?

- Can you redesign or reformulate the product to be less expensive?
- Can you re-sell what you don't use?
- Can you negotiate better prices and terms?
- Are you using a better quality than needed?
- Is there a more efficient process that would use less of the product?
- Can you dilute it more?
- Can you produce it yourself?
- Is there a different version that might actually save money because you would use much less?
- Can you get on-time delivery that would save money because you would not need as much inventory?

Now add to this list the following items:

- What are you spending on subscriptions?
- How many telephones do you really need?
- Can they be just basic rather than sophisticated?
- What are you paying in telephone bills monthly?
- Can you get better rates by shopping around a little more?
- How many of your employees really need cellular phones?
- What kind?
- Do you need all the space you are currently using?
- Do you really need a reception area and function?
- Are you better off renting rather than investing?
- Are you paying more for a centrally located facility?
- Could you be located in a less expensive area?
- How much of the travel you are paying for is unnecessary?
- Are you paying too much for office equipment maintenance contracts?
- Do local salespeople really need desks?

- How much of your office processing (such as order entry) is still done manually rather than being automated, or at least digital?
- How much of your office processing is really necessary?
- What percentage of paper reports could be reduced?
- How many people have company cars? Should they?
- How many people have expense accounts? Should they?
- How often do you review office supply contracts?
- Are there any that you can eliminate?
- How many of your people are authorized to make purchases?
- How often do you review their records?
- How many of your people are authorized for signing checks?
- How often do you review their records?
- How many computers are there in your offices?
- Do you need that many?
- How many need to be sophisticated, cutting edge technology?
- What is the percentage of usage of office computers?
- How much software do you really need?
- Which people need which kinds?
- Does anybody monitor the ways computers are being used?
- How much is office cleaning and maintenance costing?
- Are there better options?
- How many copiers do you need?
- How many printers?
- What kinds?
- Do you review expense accounts?
- Do you review sales reports?
- How many managers do you have?
- Do you need them all?
- How many administrative assistants do you have?
- Do you need them all?
- How many temporaries?

Note. Copy these lists and share them throughout the organization.

# Negotiating Checklist

Negotiating is not a topic of this book, but here are some things you may want to think about:

- Who will conduct the negotiations with the union?
- Have they had training in negotiation?
- What things have changed since the last negotiation?
- How might they affect these negotiations?
- What new issues might the union bring up?
- What have other unions in your industry and region been demanding?
- What issues do you want to bring up?
- Where do you have room to accept changes?
- What can you demand in exchange?
- What issues are critical?
- What issues are not negotiable?
- What will the cost of a new contract represent?
- At what point would a strike be preferable to an unacceptable contract?

# Interview Questions List

Of course, interviews are important to get a feeling for the human aspect of the candidate, but they should go way beyond just reviewing the resume and job history. If there was ever a time for a 360 degree evaluation, this is it. The people who will work with the candidate, both superiors and subordinates, should be given an opportunity to form and share their impressions, too.

Lots of questions can be asked.

- What didn't you like about the place where you worked before?
- What would it have taken for you to stay there?
- What different things would you like to see in our company?
- Is there anything about our company and its culture that might make you uncomfortable?
- How would you describe your management style?
- How would the people who worked with you describe it?
- What kind of management style would you prefer from your boss?
- What are your pet peeves? Why?
- What do you think of your previous bosses?
- What did they do right?
- What did they do wrong?
- What kind of boss have you worked best with?
- What are you good at?
- What things do you need to thrive in your job?
- What things are more challenging for you?
- What are some of the key lessons you have learned along the way?
- What was your favorite sport in school?
- What are your hobbies?
- What was the most difficult assignment you ever had?
- Have you ever had to fire someone?

- What was that experience like?
- What do you look for in the people who report to you? What do you do to motivate people?
- What was your favorite subject in school?
- Did you ever serve in the military? Which branch?
- What lessons did you come away with?
- Did you hold down any jobs when you were in high school or college? What kind?
- Are you in favor of change?
- Are you in favor of being changed by change?

These are just some of the questions that might help bring to light more about the candidate's character and values.

# 33 Questions You Should Ask Before You Grow Your Business Internationally

What do you need to know before you choose a specific country? These questions will help you grow your profits and avoid costly mistakes.

1. Who would be the typical users of your products in other countries?
2. What is their income?
3. How are such products priced in those countries?
4. Will your target consumers be able to afford your products?
5. What are the similarities between your products and locally available ones?
6. What are the differences?
7. Do people use them the same way?
8. Are sizes different?
9. What are the local preferences?
10. Is the same type of packaging practical?
11. Are there any social/cultural nuances related to the use of your products?
12. How are such products supplied in other countries?
13. Are there local producers of similar products? How do they compare?
14. Is the market price-oriented?
15. Who are your competitors in those markets?
16. How good are they? How well established?
17. What kinds and how much support would your products require to sell?
18. What is the typical distribution pattern in those markets?
19. What are the usual payment terms in those markets?
20. Is local financing available to you?
21. Is it available to your target distributors?
22. What would the logistics of supplying those markets involve?

23. What are the customs duties on your product if you decide to ship it into those markets?
24. If you decided to manufacture locally, would all the ingredients or components be available?
25. What are the health and consumer protection requirements of those markets?
26. What are the legal liabilities of product failure?
27. Would you need to position your product or your brand differently? How?
28. Has anyone registered your brand or a similar one in those markets?
29. Do the nations of those markets allow repatriation of profits?
30. What are the local labor laws? Would you need to change your marketing approach?
31. Would you be allowed to use the same advertising slogans and materials as in your home market?
32. How will you monitor the sale of your products?

*If you are a potential exporter and marketer of goods and services, the above questions will help you better prepare for entry into foreign markets.*

# Tip Sheet: 20 Key Questions You Need to Ask of Expat Candidates

1. Have they ever lived, or at least traveled, overseas?
2. Are they set in their ways?
3. Do they adjust easily to new circumstances?
4. Are they people-friendly?
5. Do they speak any other languages?
6. Are they capable of learning enough of the required language before going there?
7. Are their personal needs such that they can only be met in the United States?
8. Are they insightful managers and leaders?
9. Will their spouses and children be able to adjust to the new environment?
10. Can they stand the initial isolation that goes with being a foreigner in another country?
11. Are they resourceful?
12. Are they good negotiators?
13. Can they adapt and yet not go entirely native?
14. Are they good communicators?
15. Will their leadership style match the nature of local employees?
16. Are they good decision makers?
17. Do they know anything about the target country?
18. Do they have any habits or weaknesses that could get them in trouble?
19. Do they have the indispensable "street smarts" to navigate safely in a strange environment?
20. Are they good networkers?

# Puzzle Solutions

Each time you move the lines clockwise or counterclockwise, you create a new group of four numbers.

The same thing happens with the four groups of three numbers.

# About the Author

Leonardo da Vinci believed experience to be the only true source of knowledge. There truly is no substitute for experience. Michael Wynne has "walked his talk" running companies in the U.S. and abroad. He has turned businesses around in the midst of tough economic downturns; negotiated with unions in foreign countries; run manufacturing plants; worked with banks to raise funding; managed tricky government relations in several countries and taught valuable profit-making lessons that no MBA program could offer. Many of these lessons are included in this book.

From running companies, Michael learned that you cannot do it all by yourself: you need a team. Your business is only as good as the people on your team, and how well you manage them. This is the theme of the book: companies don't generate profits, people do. To achieve the ultimate excellence of Sustainable Profit Growth, everyone and everything in the company must contribute to the bottom line.

As President of International Management Consulting Associates, Michael often sees CEO's concentrate their efforts on running more efficient plants thinking it is enough to ensure greater Profit. It helps, but excellence in just one area of a business is not enough. Sustainable Profit Growth is the result of focusing all parts of the company on generating greater profits and delivering the best value to customers. This book shows readers how to achieve this great goal.

Early in his career with Mobil Oil and Mobil Chemical, Michael took a company that had been losing money for four years and turned it around in three months. He later applied the lessons from that experience to successfully manage operations in more countries. Lessons from those experiences included in this book, are The Building Blocks of Profit, The Four Avenues of Growth, and the Magic of Gross Profits.

Promoted later to Strategic Planning Manager with Mobil Chemical Company, he learned the value of both strategic and global thinking (also in the book) while developing global strategies for a $2 billion operation.

From his activities as President of non-profit professional organizations such as the National Speakers Association - Illinois, Meetings Industry Council of Chicago, and an overseas chapter of Sales and Marketing Executives International, Michael learned about motivating and working with people who do not report to you. A valuable lesson in the chapters about leadership and team building. Another lesson shared from this experience is about how we magnify one another's wisdom through collaboration as a means of achieving goals.

Over the years, Michael has coached hundreds of US and foreign executives on how to manage in different countries. This is unique in that it requires a deep understanding of management and leadership, as well as how to adapt them to the challenges of different cultures.

From his 8 years of service in the US Air Force, he learned the value of teamwork, and how to prepare people to perform well even under extremely difficult conditions. For four years Michael also taught management at Universidad Javeriana, a Jesuit university in Bogotá, Colombia. Lessons from all of the above experiences will help readers achieve the ultimate excellence of Sustainable Profit Growth.

www.ingramcontent.com/pod-product-compliance
Lightning Source LLC
Chambersburg PA
CBHW070239200326
41518CB00010B/1619